PRAISE FOR
THROWING CONFETTI

Throwing Confetti is the encouragement and inspiration our broken world needs right now. With a gentle boldness, DeAnn Carpenter invites you to step into the world of loving others the way Jesus showed us how to during His time on earth. She understands how our human hearts function and what the enemy seeks to destroy. With that knowledge, DeAnn teaches us how to train our hearts to champion, cheer, and spread hooray, both when it comes to ourselves but also for everyone we come in contact with. This book gets me so fired up and has me reaching with a giddy excitement for my bag of confetti to shower on everyone!

—LAUREN AKINS

Lauren Akins, Podcaster and Author of
Live in Love: Growing Together Through Life's Changes

I'm not a huge fan of glitter, but I do love confetti and DeAnn Carpenter! The heart behind this uplifting work is reflected in the life she lives. I know these principles and ideas will change you and your community because I've watched DeAnn display them in her daily encouragement of others and my family. Now let's go throw some confetti!

—TYLER REAGIN

Leadership Consultant; Co-Founder, The 10|TEN Project; and
Author of *Leading Things You Didn't Start*
Atlanta, Georgia

DeAnn Carpenter is a great advocate and heartfelt champion for anyone pursuing their best life. *Throwing Confetti* shows her unique ability to hold space and celebrate the people around her.

—MILES ADCOX
Chairman and Proprietor, Onsite Workshops, Nashville, Tennessee;
Co-Founder of The Oaks Center, Southern California

Throwing Confetti: Becoming a Voice of Hooray in a Hurting World is a message we need and a timely one at that. DeAnn Carpenter so beautifully lays out the need for practicing hooray and how we can get there. She lives this message and is so good at celebrating people. If you want to live in a way that is counter-cultural and choose to call out the good in others, read this book! And I pray that you would join us in honoring and cheering each other on!

—KIM WALKER-SMITH
Singer-Songwriter, Worship Leader, and Recording Artist
Redding, California

It's true that every person longs to feel seen, heard, known, and loved. In this book, DeAnn Carpenter discusses the immense value of the rhythm of celebration and its spiritual significance in understanding God's heart for humanity. *Throwing Confetti* reminds us that God desires to deliver us from a lifeless and empty existence, and when we realize what we've been rescued from, we will celebrate the Rescuer.

—CURTIS ZACKERY
Author, *Soul Rest: Reclaim Your Life. Return to Sabbath*
Franklin, Tennessee

We don't drift toward hooray and hallelujah. This is the message for all of us whose thought lives are dripping with comparison or cynicism. There is another way (a better way). We are all longing for a world of hooray, Eden really. DeAnn Carpenter walks us through how to take, albeit imperfect, steps toward authentic celebration in the midst of a hurting world.

—REBECCA GEORGE
Author, Speaker; Podcast Host of *Radical Radiance*
Brookhaven, Mississippi

There are encouragers in life, and then if you're lucky, you'll encounter a "Yoda of hooray," and their words aren't just encouragement, their life is. DeAnn Carpenter is every bit that Yoda. I met her in a drought of joy, and she lit a spark in my soul. This book is a collection of the embers she exudes in her own life. As you read these words, I pray that your life is impacted by her evident time in God's presence and the kindness and compassion she truly walks in.

—CHARISE OROZCO
Author; Teacher; Co-Pastor, Liberty Church
St. Petersburg, Florida

DeAnn has written a book that I believe is perfect for a post-pandemic society. If you've been prone to cynicism or simply have struggled to see the good in the midst of the bad, this book is for you!

—TIM ROSS
Pastor, Embassy City Church
Irving, Texas

DeAnn Carpenter's critically important book is a timely reminder that an echo of heaven is revealed in the chorus of our voices, united, cheering on the individual races we are called to run.

—ROGER W. THOMPSON
Author, *We Stood Upon Stars: Finding God in Lost Places*
and *My Best Friend's Funeral: A Memoir*
Ventura, California

In a world where people are constantly beat up and put down, *Throwing Confetti* is both a timely and timeless message. DeAnn Carpenter's style is honest, engaging, insightful, winsome, and fun! She does a masterful job of helping us overcome the lack of hooray in our lives so that we can become world-class confetti throwers. I promise you this book will inspire you to pick up handfuls of confetti and start spreading hooray everywhere you go.

—LANCE WITT
Founder, Replenish Ministries
Castle Rock, Colorado

THROWING

Confetti

THROWING

BECOMING A VOICE
OF HOORAY
IN A HURTING WORLD

By
DeAnn K. Carpenter

RESOURCES

CONTENTS

PART 2: CAPES & CAMOUFLAGE

PART 3: BOORAY

PART 4: THE GIANT OF SMALLNESS

PART 5: LOST IN TRANSLATION

PART 6: FAN CLUB

PART 7: CONFETTI MESSES

PART 8: STANDING NEXT TO STRENGTH

PART 9: PARTS + PIECES + PRACTICES

PART 10: RULING & REIGNING

To Our Refuge Staff

To those in the past who have tilled a hard ground beside us. To the ones who stand beside us now. And to those on the horizon who will come and join our rodeo. This book is our heartbeat. This book is for you.

Only God knows the depths of your sacrifice to serve the saints. I can't imagine what you have coming; your crown will be so big. How good is God that He would place you with us. I am overwhelmed.

I have been on teams my entire life, and you are my most favorite people to play, serve, and lead beside. Your service is the embodiment of *hooray*. Every time you give, confetti flies. And we never mind the mess. Love you.

To Brian Carpenter

Only because of your dreaming, risk-taking, and obedience is there a place for us to serve and sacrifice together at Refuge. Your vision has always seen the path our feet should take. I am in awe.

You are a giant ball of confetti and that's at least half of the reason why I have something to say. It's not fair that you're mine. I love, love, love you.

Dear Reader

Our world needs more cheering and less condemning.
More rejoicing, less rejecting.
More delighting in, less denouncing of.
More confetti, less critique.
More applause, more bravo, more hooray.

We each have been given the divine ability to help shift the narrative for people by what we say and how we see. It's with that in mind that I submit to you this book, praying that God will take these words and translate them to fit you uniquely. I hope it will impact how you interact with God, how you champion others, and how you cheer for those closest to you. And, I sincerely hope no one gets blown away by all the confetti you start to throw. I simply can't be held responsible for that.

FOREWORD

The first time I met DeAnn Carpenter, I immediately picked up on her friendliness and welcoming demeanor. But what really stood out to me was her genuine cheerfulness. In our first conversations, she made me feel like she was completely for me. It wasn't my reputation or because of what I have accomplished, but simply because that is who she is. Her warmth, words, and expression all throw shiny confetti that screams, *I believe in you!*

I've spent enough time with DeAnn now to realize that I am not the only one who gets to see and experience this. DeAnn is an incredible cheerleader to everyone around her. While she's frank and doesn't mince words, she calls out the good, the prophetic, and the truth.

Throwing Confetti is a message the world needs and a timely one at that. DeAnn so beautifully lays out the need for practicing *hooray* and how to get there in your own life. She and her husband, Brian, truly live this message and are some of the very best at celebrating people. I pray that as you read this book, you would feel confetti leap off the pages. I pray that areas in your own heart, where negative words have left a painful scar, would be healed as Jesus meets you in this message. Lastly, I pray that you would join us in honoring and cheering each other on!

In a world where we are bombarded with various social media platforms constantly tugging at our thoughts and emotions, tempting us to compare and criticize, we need a new message. The rise of cancel culture and an overarching need to prove oneself are wreaking havoc on so many lives. Jealousy and comparison are the greatest thieves of creativity. What if we decided that enough is enough? What if we determined in ourselves that we want a new standard?

We need people like DeAnn, who are intentional with their words and make a point to delight in others. After all, this should be the heart of a true leader, mother, or father. We want to see those that we lead go beyond us. The happiest leaders are the ones who know how to serve, cheer, and call out the best in those they are serving. These are the kind of leaders we trust and are drawn to follow and learn from.

Can you imagine a world where we celebrate each other and call out the good in each person? That is a world that I want to live in! With love and confetti, I am happy to introduce you to a leader I trust, my good friend with a great message, DeAnn Carpenter.

—Kim Walker-Smith
Singer-Songwriter,
Worship Leader and
Recording Artist

PROLOGUE

First, I think heaven will be full of confetti. Divine sparkle every-where reflecting the Father of Lights Himself. The streets of gold, the choirs of angels, and wonder around every corner. But no gluten-free options, obviously, because we will be fully satisfied for all time.

Second, I believe it is both our job and privilege to pull pieces of heaven down to earth so that each of us can experience and extend the eternal beauty and shine it offers.

How do we do that?

One approach to practicing *hooray* is to partner with the Holy Spirit. That union allows us to *see people the way He sees them* and then release His message. It's a sacred work to cheer and genuinely celebrate a hurting world. When we applaud and honor a child of God, when we use our mouths to bless and build up rather than tear down, then light-filled divine confetti makes its way down to hearts here on earth, planting its divine seed.

Does this sound cotton candy–headed or like a Pollyanna style of living? That's never been me. After all, I'm a type 8 on the Enneagram. But you don't have to be a certain Enneagram number or a specific category on a StrengthsFinder test, an extrovert versus an introvert, or whatever to participate. It just is living and loving on the same basis we see throughout Jesus's life. (We'll look more deeply into that later.)

Throwing confetti helps change people's negative narratives from weak to strong, invisible to invincible, beaten down to beloved. Not only is the power of the positive modeled in the Bible, it is supported by science as well.

Modern researchers have established that the human brain is more sensitive to unpleasant things. Downbeat news influences our attitudes more heavily than upbeat news. This has been called the *negativity bias*. Scientists also have established this principle: for a positive experience to stick in our memory, we have to focus on it for ten to twenty seconds. Otherwise we'll forget it. In other words, it takes more work to be influenced by the positive than the negative.

But the advantages are many, according to decades of research (and common sense). For example, having a positive outlook produces less stress, better physical and emotional health, better coping skills, and a longer life span.

So, the practice of *hooray* is important to our personal mental, emotional, and spiritual health. But it's of course more than that. Having God's lens will widen our view as we see others as souls who are made in His image, who hold incredible value and were created to offer something beautiful to the world. Honestly, that's enough to clap about on any day.

I believe that people who partner with God hold the keys to Spirit-led encouragement. We have to start unlocking it in greater ways because a comparative and competitive lens is blurring the view for many in our culture. There are also plenty of other hurdles to our hallelujah choruses because our world is fallen and people are hurting.

If our churches, schools, social media platforms, and workplaces could extend cheer and applause like we currently offer criticism, intolerance, and judgment, we might just be rolling in confetti. But we're not; we're knee-deep in something else.

I think it's time we make a change. If we all just shift a little, we could have monumental impact on each other. So I wonder if we could keep our hearts open as we explore *hooray* from the original Author (that's God) and rid ourselves of the things that stand in the way of our applause toward others. Our cheering for another person's place in life will keep the encores loud in their heart and their feet steady on the ground. We all benefit when there is strength beside us.

In our family life, we try to steward confetti by helping our kids to understand that our differences and uniquenesses are to be celebrated, that we are to be each other's loudest and best cheerleaders as we champion the uniqueness God has put inside of us. Some days the kids even rally to do it. More often, though, they're in their bedrooms writing apologies or taking a time-out because, for most of us, *hooray* is not a natural part of our DNA. It takes work to use our voices to bless and lift our hands to clap, and at eight and ten they are still working out a lot of kinks.

Okay, at forty their mom is still working out some of the kinks too.

We get plenty of chances to practice, though. My husband and I run an organization (https://refuge.rest) whose sole purpose is to be *hooray* for weary leaders. Leading is hard and only getting harder. If our good leaders give up, our world suffers. We throw confetti as we honor and serve the people who are taking care of people. We get behind these leaders with a phenomenal staff to facilitate reprieve so they can continue to move forward, make an impact, and keep the confetti falling for others.

I'll forewarn you, before we jump in, that *hooray* can't be faked or prefabricated. Also, sometimes confetti leaves a real mess. I'm being blunt, I know. I've always been a truth-teller to a fault. It takes work to cheer and it takes time to champion people, and it's the kind of work we need to do alongside one another as we extend the gifts that are within us.

By the way, the book isn't set up in a typical way. I'm a little outside the box, so my book is too! You'll see parts instead of chapters, and each part has a collection of "readings" under a unifying theme. Each part ends with a meditation and a verse or two to reflect on.

So grab yourself some pom-poms, take a good look at who's next to you, and get in step with the Spirit, because there are people who need the exclamation your voice holds and the cheer your life can extend.

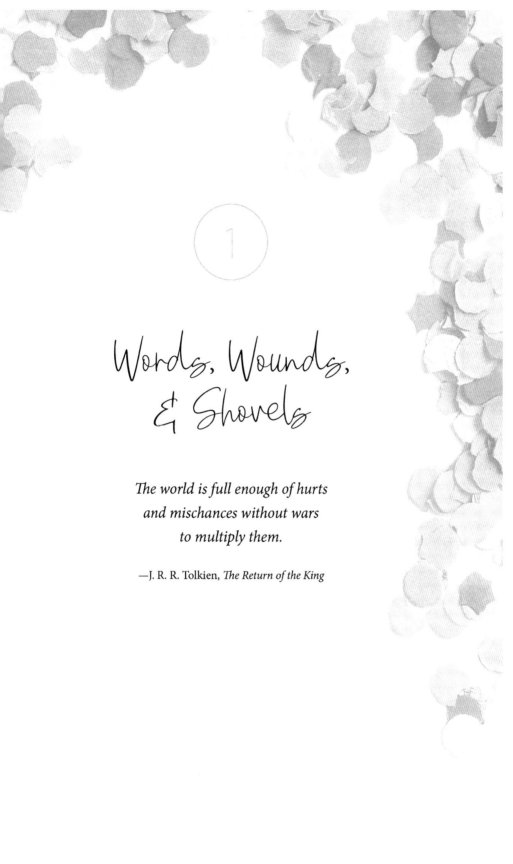

Words, Wounds, & Shovels

*The world is full enough of hurts
and mischances without wars
to multiply them.*

—J. R. R. Tolkien, *The Return of the King*

SEEING THE WRINKLES

My husband has been wearing glasses since the second grade. Back then he was really something, in his short shorts and with bottlecap glasses on his sweet face.

Today, his prescription is as powerful as it can be. Any further improvement would need to involve surgery. I for one hate needles, so I can't imagine volunteering to let a doctor poke around my eyeball with one. However, I understand the necessity. Last week Brian asked me if his gray shirt, which was clearly green and very wrinkled, was too wrinkled to wear.

It made me think how some of us have gotten so comfortable with the point of view we have toward others, and maybe even toward ourselves, that we don't even notice the wrinkling through our lens, or how it's affecting our sight. *How* we see is so important. It determines the views we hold; it filters what we perceive to be true.

I wonder if some good poking around might be worthwhile as we examine in this book how throwing confetti can have great benefit for us and for those who stand next to us.

Sure, it can be uncomfortable, but who doesn't want more clarity?

FIRST THINGS FIRST

It's hard to know where to start when you decide to write a book. So I thought I'd just start at the beginning, with what happened first.

We usually remember our "firsts." The first date, the first kiss, or the first time we fell in love. There are other firsts too, of course. The first time we got made fun of, our first breakup, our first real heartache. There are all kinds of firsts in life. If we dwell on them long enough, it can move us toward delight, or despair.

So I thought that if we are going to have hearts that issue *hooray*— if we are going to learn how best to throw confetti—we ought to look at God's firsts, first.

The first thing God says. The first people He lets walk and talk with Him and learn from Him. The first sin and how He responds. The first kids He allows to be born outside of Eden. The first king He sets up to rule His people. This is where we'll see how *hooray* got its beginning, where it collapsed, and why it's so important for us to pick it up and partner with it.

Let's start in Genesis. We see God generously *extending*. He extended beauty, breath, and life. This is where *hooray* was first issued.

In the beginning God chose to create something where there was nothing—by using His words. His words were so powerful that, once spoken, the nothing became substance, which materialized into something. Genesis is where God extended His breath to our first parents, Adam and Eve. They were made in the image of God by the breath of God.

As image bearers like Eve and Adam, all of us are still forming our futures because of what's being extended and spoken over each other. Following God's pattern, we all are using our breath to breathe life into people and using our lives to help lift people. This was God's intention from the beginning, so I reckon it should be something we need to practice. Hence this book.

THE POWER OF WORDS

Adam and Eve were created with ears to hear *hooray* from the One Who authored it. Now, I for one can't imagine a scene where walking naked among animals is the norm. But the Bible makes it clear that things in Eden were really good—until a snake showed up and started talking.

He slithered his way into the third chapter of Genesis where he began using twisted rhetoric to spin God's words with our first mother. Eve had no experience with deceit or how to navigate a twisted wordsmith. So she was baited until she bit.

Notice something here. God came in the beginning with His words. The enemy *also* came with words. But instead of using them to create life, he used them to destroy it. The snake tempted Eve by distorting God's words and spinning a crafty web of distortions. *Did God really say . . . ? No, He didn't . . . That isn't true . . . You won't die . . .*

It worked.

> When the woman saw that the fruit of the tree was good for food and pleasing to the eye, and also desirable for gaining wisdom, she took some and ate it. She also gave some to her husband, who was with her, and he ate it. (Genesis 3:6)

And so went the fall of humankind.

Our beginning went sideways because of words that were twisted, words that were then believed by our first parents. What we do with words and what we believe about the words that are being spoken to us will have monumental effects on our life.

HOORAY WOULD HAVE HELPED

Truthfully, I think chocolate would have made more sense. It has always been hard for my mind to envision how a fruit caused the fall of humanity. But chocolate? If I were Eve, my mantra of *Don't touch the Tree! Don't touch the Tree! Don't touch the Tree!* would have barely lasted a couple of days. The snake would not have been needed.

Either way, "the lust of the flesh, the lust of the eyes, and the pride of life," as John calls it in 1 John 2:16, were now in play, not only as a temptation for Adam and Eve but for all of us.

I find it interesting that the snake, being the most "crafty," uses *comparison* as the hook that baited Eve and tempted her to take what wasn't supposed to be hers.

> "You will not certainly die," the serpent said to the woman. "For God knows that when you eat from it your eyes will be opened, and you will be like God, knowing good and evil." (Genesis 3:4-5)

"You will be like God . . ." I'm guessing that the serpent knew Eve already had compared herself to her Creator—and was not content with the realization that she wasn't as powerful as God. She wanted to be like God, not like herself.

And because of that—because of trying to be "like" someone else—some key part of her died.

The score was now Snake: 1, Humanity: 0.

Eve was the first to believe a bad word. The thought was planted in her mind that she could be more, more like God, and she was deceived that she *needed* to be more. So Eve reached for what God said was forbidden.

Then she decided to share the bite. I don't know if Eve even paused before she offered the fruit to Adam. Scripture doesn't give us the details. After doing the wrong thing, did she think about rooting for Adam to do the right thing? Did she consider telling her husband to flee? She had a plethora of other choices: she could have run fast to God and confessed; she could have even jumped on a giraffe and ridden for a while to clear her head. We don't know what she was thinking.

All we know is that she offered Adam a bite, and he ate.

Snake: 2, Humanity: 0

Then, after they ate, their eyes were "opened" and their spirits were heavy with guilt. They went and found a bush and got down real low, because guilt, shame, and disappointment do not call any of us to stand upright. They cause us to cower.

But it's hard to hide from a God Who already sees us completely. He knows every word before we say it, every thought before we think it, and of course every place where we stand or crouch in to hide.

When God caught up to the cowering couple, He asked Adam why he was in hiding. Adam's response was, "I was afraid because I was naked; so I hid" (Genesis 3:10).

That's a trait that's been passed down to us from our first parents and tucked deep into our hearts. It's why we need to deal with the things that are keeping us hidden. If we don't come out of hiding, whatever the reasons are, then *hooray* is going to be really hard for us.

HOW *HOORAY* GETS HELD UP

That is our beginning, a beautiful word extended by God that brought life and a bad word offered to Eve that issued death. The words we offer to others have impact not only for a moment or a season but for a lifetime; we'd be wise to be really careful with them.

It's all detailed in Genesis, how the first couple deals with the first account of social distancing and finds themselves outside the doors of Eden in a new place to rest and work. Eventually they start having kids. Cain and Abel become some of the very first offspring after the fall. Their story provides us with dramatic details of why confetti can be so hard for us. It's the first account of how *hooray* literally goes to the grave.

We pick up the story in Genesis 4, and might I also say, *What in the world?* The account never fails to stop me in my tracks.

> The man was intimate with his wife Eve, and she conceived and gave birth to Cain. . . . She also gave birth to his brother Abel. Now Abel became a shepherd of flocks, but Cain worked the ground. In the course of time Cain presented some of the land's produce as an offering to the LORD. And Abel also presented an offering—some of the firstborn of his flock and their fat portions. The LORD had regard for Abel and his offering, but he did not have regard for Cain and his offering. Cain was furious, and he looked despondent. (Genesis 4:1-5 CSB)

By verse 8, instead of sifting through the whispers in his head and lifting his hands to clap for his brother, Cain reaches (maybe) for a shovel. He invites Abel to his field and kills him!

Friends, if our emotions are calling the shots, it does not take long for those feelings to hold us hostage. Cain ends up digging to bury something. Unfortunately, he chose his brother and not his pride.

WHAT HAPPENED?

Why couldn't Cain just clap for his brother's success? Why did Cain think that Abel's offering reflected at all on him? Their portions were different; what they had to offer God was different too. Cain could have learned something by looking at his brother's offering. But the wrong lens kept things out of focus.

People still get caught up in the shenanigans of sibling rivalry, of course, and worse. If we can't learn how to celebrate our differences and applaud each other's unique strengths and portions, then we will disintegrate into the noisy chaos, the belittling newsfeeds, and the unfortunate game of comparison this world is bent on playing. Comparison, envy, jealousy, and a competition mindset of "I need to be better than you" will keep us from being a people who can throw confetti. It will keep our voices from cheering and bring *hooray* to a halt in us. When you are holding a shovel, it limits what else you can carry.

I believe these feelings to be the fruit of a condition I call "lack."

Lack is where we find ourselves believing that who we are in our uniqueness just isn't enough for some reason. So we try to prove lack wrong by being more, having more, or trying to do more than others. Trying to be "better than" steals our cheer and limits how well we champion others because our eyes are focused only on ourselves. Lack will limit what we can see in others.

LIMITS & LACK

I can't help but think that lack was set into motion right after Adam took the bite and decided to hide with Eve.

Remember, when God made His way toward Adam and Eve, He asked an important question: "Who told you that you were naked?" (Genesis 3:11). The two humans now perceived that they were *missing* something. They came to believe that they were without something essential, and in need of something more.

Lack happens when we take our eyes off our Creator and start taking measurements of what God has *created* instead of what He has *said*. Looking around us can limit us. When we seek to compare ourselves to what others have or who they are, we can start to feel like we are coming up short. But we weren't created to be the same as the next guy. Any comparisons we make to others will already be off-kilter. Our authenticity will be at war with insecurity.

And I want to point out that *having* less is much different than inherently *being* less. And if having less makes you feel like you *are* less, then, friend, your view is skewed.

Although comparisons feel tangible, they're not real. If we allow our view of others to set a standard for who we are supposed to be, then we've picked up lack as our lens.

Eve wanted to be more like God. She reached for the fruit, thinking she would acquire what she thought she lacked. That choice, though, ended in true lack: the loss of innocence, the end of intimacy with the Creator, work and childbirth transformed into sweat and pain, all subsequent generations doomed to sin.

I believe we are all fighting the battle of lack or limit to some extent because Adam and Eve *felt* much less after God issued the judgment for the sin that took place in Eden. We've been chasing after pre-fall Eden ever since, trying to fulfill ourselves with things never meant to fully satisfy. Lack is usually an underlying condition. Its symptoms can include feelings of intimidation, smallness, jealousy, envy, and anger.

Lack will choke your voice until you're too constrained to say anything good, let alone yell *hooray*. This kind of mindset limits us from seeing and applauding what God has put inside of another. Lack is the very idea that makes war with *hooray* because the nature of measurement is contradictory to the portions God has given us. Until we settle into who we are, the gifts we have, and the uniqueness that's solely ours to express, applauding and offering anything to others will be very difficult.

We are all carrying something uniquely different and beautiful. Something that's only ours to give. Don't downplay what you have because you're looking at the different portions around you. God doesn't make measurements about what He gives to us based on what others have or who they are. He gives to us accordingly, uniquely, and purposefully. He is a good giver. What He has for you is far better than what you could try to get for yourself. Just ask Eve.

WITHHOLDING WON'T HELP

So as we've seen, Eve's son Cain made his measurements out of lack by looking at his brother. Abel brought his best, but Cain held back from God. Then Cain got angry with Abel, because Abel's generous heart made Cain look bad.

But listen, we don't end up with more when we withhold from God or others. In fact, it's the exact opposite. I love Luke 6:38. "When we give, it will be given back to us with a generous heaping of more" (my translation!). Withholding won't give us more; in the end we will end up with less.

This truth should make the believers of God the most generous people of all. We are a people that have received the most generous words to share, things to offer, and lives to extend. But oftentimes, like Cain, we withhold.

I'm sure Cain could conjure up all kinds of reasons why he did what he did. We don't have a lot of context for how these boys were raised. Did they grow up in a household where teamwork and cheer were encouraged? I would guess not. I imagine, after being thrown out of the garden, Adam and Eve still had a lot to work through as they raised their kids and got used to a hard life where God was not as tangible as He was in Eden.

The Bible only brings us up to speed about these boys' growth from birth to adulthood with one tiny phrase: "in the course of time" (Genesis 4:3 CSB). So we don't have any details about the experiences that would lead Cain to hold back and hoard things for himself. At any rate his thoughts became the breeding ground for his emotions to feed off, and like any sickness that has no remedy, things started to spread.

If I'm reading the narrative correctly, there were not many people alive on the planet for Cain to compare himself to. However, one person is all that's needed for us to make a mess with the measuring line.

When Cain didn't measure himself by the right One, the world's first case of murder was set into motion. Lack, jealousy, envy, and all kinds of other underlying emotions kept heavenly confetti from falling. And here's another point. After Cain killed Abel, he dug a hole and laid the body in the dirt. Like his mom and dad, Cain tried to hide from God what he had just done (see Genesis 4:9).

You would think that's one lesson he would have learned from his parents. Hiding never helps anyone escape from God.

UNIQUELY YOURS

What each of us has to offer God and each other has nothing to do with what others have or what they do with what they have. We are only accountable for what we are given. We can only offer and sacrifice what God puts in our lives.

Cain's offering didn't need to look like his brother's. It would have matched the work that God gave him to do. However, comparison doesn't value what we do have to bring. It only focuses on and exaggerates what isn't ours—what we lack.

Cain withheld from God by only bringing *some* of what he had to offer. Something that was less generous and something that was smaller than he was capable of extending. He kept a portion to himself. Instead of growing up in the call to become more, which is often hard for us, he grabbed a shovel and took another route that didn't require any more measuring. Instead of tossing the measuring stick and rallying for his brother, he was slinging dirt and wallowing.

If we can't come to terms with the strengths and portions that God gives to others, then comparison will crush us, if not completely end us. Comparison has caused a collapse in *hooray* because when we are constantly assessing self, there is little room to celebrate others. The only reason we should need a shovel is to uncover the good that has been buried under the mess of debris that pain, lack, and comparison leave on a heart.

NEW & NOW

We've looked at God's first act, the first image bearers, the first kids, and then where *hooray* first fell. There's one more story about firsts we need to take a look at.

This is the first time that God named a king. Turns out, like Adam and Eve, this king also struggled with hiding. But *hooray* was used to bring him out.

In 1 Samuel 9 the nation of Israel was asking for something new. God is not opposed to new. It's His nature. What the nation was really wanting, though, wasn't new; it was similar. They wanted to be like everyone else. All the other nations in the region had kings, so they asked God to give them a king that they could follow, even though God warned them (in 1 Samuel 8) that it might turn out badly.

God's spokesperson, a prophet named Samuel, had God's specific directions to find Saul and make him king. Saul was shocked! He protested that his tribe was the smallest of all Israel's tribes, and not only that, his family was the least important in the tribe (see 1 Samuel 9:21). He did not grow up dreaming of a crown on his head.

That may be why, on the day of coronation, Saul was nowhere to be found. I get why Saul—following Eve, Adam, and Cain (and by then, others on a very long list)—decided to disappear. Thankfully, nothing is hidden before God. He revealed to Samuel that the hidden king was hiding among the baggage (see 1 Samuel 10:22).

New things can be scary! If the *hoorays* from the Holy Spirit and other places haven't reached our hearts, the instinct to hide is understandable. When we don't feel like we have what it takes, we can hide in all kinds of ways. Unless we rid ourselves of the old baggage we are carrying, it will remain a place that's comfortable for us to return to again and again. Which means we can't offer *hooray* or anything else for that matter if we insist on hiding.

UNPACK IT

Baggage is heavy. If you've ever had to make a run for it to get to your boarding gate on time, you know this concept well. We move easier when we aren't tied down with weight. Unpacking is the only way to travel lightly into our future.

Eventually each of us has to say goodbye to old habits, mindsets, and ways of coping in order to get settled into the new things that God has for us. Samuel said of Saul that "there is no one like him among all the people" (1 Samuel 10:24). Does that sound like a man who ought to be hiding in baggage?

Saul wasn't leaping on stage or posting news about his new position because, like many of us, what he thought of himself did not match who God said he was. Do you know people like that? Courageous, strong, and gifted with something to say or something to do but they're tucked away somewhere believing they don't have what it takes to step into new places.

The truth is that we don't always know the lens that people see through. We don't know all the data he had on himself nor do we know how he viewed God exactly or the kind of framework his upbringing gave him on those matters. What we do know is that when God called him into more, he was found hiding, and that is a familiar feeling.

There is a great chasm between who we know ourselves to be and who God says we are. I believe that when we adopt *hooray* and start throwing confetti at others, we will start closing the gap on these two things.

HURTING & HIDING

When there hasn't been healing from past hurt or pain, it will stifle our applause over others and limit our view of ourselves. It's hard to see, much less applaud, other people when our own hearts are hurting or compromised. Each of us will need to unpack and put down the things standing in our way—things that are still withholding us from forward movement, from taking our place, and from offering our portion.

My suitcase was getting heavy by the fourth grade. I had finally found a friend to hang out with that wasn't a boy. I was really excited to have a new gal pal who was just as excited about playing sports at recess as I was. Not many of the other girls were up for competitive play, so we always joined in with the boys for team sports. I will humbly tell you that I had a fantastic arm and fast feet, so if I ever got picked third, it felt like last to me.

My new friend took quick notice and didn't take a liking to either my athletic ability or my fourth-grade beauty. I'll note I was the only one in the class who could get my hair as high as Cyndi Lauper's (this was in the eighties!). Were they jealous? You bet, but not the smart ones. Soon, news about my new nickname, "Dogface," had spread even to the upper grades. It stuck around way longer than I would've liked. I no longer had to worry about getting picked third at recess because for the rest of the year I wasn't getting picked at all.

That was the first time I realized our strength can be a problem for other people. Whether it's accusation or applause that's coming our way, we have to know what to unpack and what to carry because words will change us. They will change how we see someone else and how we see ourselves.

Heavy words spoken over you will make it hard to speak good words over others. Words will mess with your measuring system, how you measure yourself because of a word or how you measure others based on whispers. All that measuring can make a person dizzy because just like when you look through a kaleidoscope, the patterns of culture and the opinions of others will always be shifting. Words need to be weighed by us, and honestly I don't know many people who want extra weight hanging onto them that's not proving to be useful.

Some of us may grow up, but we don't grow out of that mentality, still getting lost in a looking glass. That's a hard way to live, making your measurement by what others say, what you see, or how well you stand up next to other people. It's like going through your life walking on a high wire trying to keep your balance, but the problem is that the next time opinions change, you'll find yourself up there wavering without a comfortable landing. That's not only silly, it's dangerous.

THE TRADE

I have a friend who recently ran a hundred miles in a month. *One hundred miles in just a month.* I was stunned when she told me, and I started feeling a little bad about myself. I thought, *She is really amazing. I wish I could run one hundred miles.*

Did I tell her that? Eventually. But for too long I wrestled with all the thoughts that plagued me due to comparison. *I don't have as much time as she has. . . . I have a lot more responsibilities. . . . She is more disciplined than me. . . .* Then there was this kicker: *I would like to get toned but don't want to have to run to do it, but if I don't do it, I won't look as good as her . . . and it's swimsuit season.*

Jealousy was starting to pile so high I could barely see straight, let alone put my hands together to make any noise for her. My lens wasn't being filtered through her strength and accomplishment, or through God and how He saw her—just through my judgmental self-perception. And it was getting harder and harder to see as I shrunk.

The best part about this ridiculous dialogue that I had with only myself was that no one was actually asking me to run one hundred miles. Therefore, thankfully, I didn't have to say no. I had no audience around me wondering if I was even capable of it. My friend's run had *nothing to do with me.*

Well, deep exhale here because it's that truth that makes us free to look at others without comparison or measurement with ourselves.

It makes us free to cheer, and it opens us up to applaud at all times. We are not built the same, praise God.

We all have to make deliberate daily choices to toss the shovel and grab something heavier—the megaphone—in order to give something good away to the people around us that we are called to cheer for. That's the trade.

A REMEDY

We all have to wrestle with ourselves until *hooray* becomes a natural part of how we see, speak, and act.

The truth is, I don't have much to offer anyone until I've spent time with Him. I'm only scratching the surface when it comes to the depths of my selfishness. I wake up in the morning thinking about what I need, hoping I have enough coffee to get me there.

So I need to intentionally listen to and talk with His Spirit and let Him guide my heart and mind back toward what is good and true. Because celebrating God's wonderful and weird people (me included) takes work, at least for me. We will have to make choices that bend our will so that we act in the best interest of others. Even if it feels contrary at times.

You need to practice. Create your own mantra. Write it down, speak it out, say it until you believe it, and keep saying it until you are living it. As you start every day, make a declaration. Put into words what you need to see happen. Here's an example.

> *I will choose to cheer for another. I will cheer for their blessing, whether or not I see my own. I will applaud their work, whether I'm excelling or struggling. I will give voice to all the good things God has for them, no matter my circumstances. I won't hide when others shine; I won't hide so that others can shine. I will offer, receive, and applaud my portion and the portion others have been given.*

Bottom line: the best way to stir up cheer and throw confetti for others is to have more of God. God's lens, God's heart, God's Word—guiding and applying it to your life. Directing your steps, your heart, and your mouth.

A NEW WORD

Here's the thing about words. What makes them so powerful is what we choose to believe about them, and what we believe about the One Who authored them.

If we don't unpack and let go of old words and painful wounds, they stay with us like old weight we can't get off. But when we bring our hurt to the altar to be dealt with and ask God for a new word, a better word, then it brings us out from hiding.

I am in desperate need of His heart and His mind working through me. I have to daily get before God and let His Spirit gently guide and correct my thoughts so that I'm aligned with Him and measuring my day by what He says and not by what I see.

When we stay connected to His Spirit, it affects our spirits, and when our hearts are continually affected by Him, then change can happen. When you are personally settled by the things He's said over you and the things that are still being whispered to you, then you'll start to find yourself more at rest in your divine uniqueness. The more settled in you are, the easier extending to others becomes. You never know who is going to need your extension.

Thank goodness Saul, playing hide-and-seek, had some people in his corner who knew how to lend a hand and be a voice. Saul's future was in serious limbo. After Saul was found hiding, the text notes that others went and got him. These are some of my favorite words in the Bible. The text actually says these cheerleaders *ran to Saul*. "They ran and brought him out" (1 Samuel 10:23).

They wasted no time. They thought not of themselves. And despite a man who was about to be the first king hiding in baggage, they didn't yell judgments of his inadequacies—because he was who God picked.

They ran to the corner and brought him out so that he could take his place, and now the tears are coming because what a thing to do. I wonder what they said. What words were on their lips that convinced a man who thought he was small to step forward into one of the highest ruling positions there was?

What I do know is that when God breathes on the words we say, those words become something of substance in us, pieces of confetti that land on our hearts and stick to our spirits.

Meditation

My husband is still wearing glasses, by the way. Actually, his vision has improved because of them. How about that. The right lens will enhance your perception and correct your view.

Metaphorically, he's so good at seeing people through a lens that's bigger, more generous, and so accurate that he's made a career out of confetti throwing. When we improve our lens, it's not only better for us but also for those next to us.

You and I were made in the image of God; we were given the ability to speak life into places and people. There are places and people around us that need our applause today, people who won't ask for confetti, but if it's extended to them, it could change how they shine. These people may be on the stage, tucked in a corner, or next to you on your spin bike. Their strength is from God and for your benefit, so start clapping. You offer it from a place of plenty; you *are* enough and you *have* enough to offer.

So with that in mind, let's ponder some thoughts:
- Is there any place in your life that comparison has set in, hindering you or getting in the way of your being able to clap and admire?
- What are some of your strengths?
- Are you intentional with the words you're speaking and the words you are believing?

REFLECTION

"Pleasant words are a honeycomb, sweet to the soul and healing to the bones." (Proverbs 16:24 NASB)

"I am about to do something new. See, I have already begun!
Do you not see it? I will make a pathway through the wilderness.
I will create rivers in the dry wasteland." (Isaiah 43:19 NLT)

2

Capes & Camouflage

Be weird. Be random.
Be who you are.
Because you never know
who would love the
person you hide.

—Unknown

TO SHINE

I am constantly surrounded by camouflage. It's the nature of the nonprofit my husband and I run. In the fall I can look out the lodge's windows, and if I didn't know any better, I'd think the trees decided to get up and go for a walk. But no, it's our clients and staff, covered head to toe in camo.

The gear you wear matters, especially if you plan to catch the fish or kill the game. You cannot be seen. It's a good trick, really, to be in plain sight and still not be noticed. Hunting blinds and disguises have been helping millions get away with this kind of clever maneuvering for forever.

It's easy to find an analogy here, isn't it? I can't help but think of all the ways in life we try to blend in, if not hide ourselves, all the while being right there in the open. I'm not saying there aren't plenty of reasons for this. But given that light is supposed to shine, I just don't see it as God's idea.

Light is supposed to offer something to others. Light helps us see and find our way. Light extends something to us, opens something up for us, and offers illumination to those who would otherwise be stumbling. A space that is filled with darkness is only transformed when light is present.

WE'VE GOT A RUNNER

Sarai, wife to Abram—who would become Abraham, the patriarch of Judaism, Christianity, and Islam—felt like she was in a tight spot. God had promised in Genesis 15:4 that Abram would have a son, which meant Sarai would bear a child. But her biological clock was ticking. Let's be honest, it was way outta time. Sarai decided she had to form a plan to help God out.

I feel like Sarai took matters into her own hands because no one was throwing any confetti her way by speaking words that would lift her spirits and remind her that God always comes through on His promises. At least, the Bible doesn't tell us of anyone doing so. No support, no encouragement, no reassurance. When we don't have arms to collapse into, we can be prone to busy our hands by plotting.

And what a plot.

> Now Sarai, Abram's wife, had not been able to bear children for him. But she had an Egyptian servant named Hagar. So Sarai said to Abram, "The LORD has prevented me from having children. Go and sleep with my servant. Perhaps I can have children through her." And Abram agreed with Sarai's proposal. So Sarai, Abram's wife, took Hagar the Egyptian servant and gave her to Abram as a wife. (Genesis 16:1-3 NLT)

At first the plan looked like it was going to work fabulously. Hagar indeed became pregnant. But for whatever reason, Hagar began to despise Sarai. Their relationship went south fast. Sarai had tried to force Hagar into a position as head cheerleader by being the baby carrier for the family, but Hagar wasn't staying in formation, and Sarai was angry and hurt and bent on revenge. She went complaining to Abram.

> Then Sarai said to Abram, "This is all your fault! I put my servant into your arms, but now that she's pregnant she treats me with contempt. The LORD will show who's wrong—you or me!" Abram replied, "Look, she is your servant, so deal with her as you see fit." Then Sarai treated Hagar so harshly that she finally ran away. (Genesis 16:5-6 NLT)

I feel like Sarai didn't think her plan through very well. Hindsight can be a hard teacher. How many times have you taken things into your own hands, made your own plans, and then blamed someone else for it? I confess I have plenty of personal examples. We are a people bent on getting what we want even if it will cost us, am I right?

On a side note, this drama happened before God changed this gal's name: from *Sarai* (quarrelsome) to *Sarah* (princess). Maybe you've known people at a point in their story before God changed their name, their identity. They weren't free; they weren't happy, whole, or healthy. Their name hadn't yet moved from tragic to beloved, from barren to full, from desperate to hopeful, from oppressed to liberated.

Bless those people who knew us before we ourselves underwent such a transformation and who now have eyes to see our new identity! Sometimes we keep people locked into a label, even though they've gone through transformation. We'd be smart to see people for who they are today and wise to see them for who they could be tomorrow.

In the case with poor Hagar, she had the misfortune of knowing quarrelsome Sarai before her identity was changed to God's princess—before she was full in her faith and just plain full of life. So let's go easy on her.

WHERE DID THE LIGHT GO?

As we saw in the Garden of Eden, running and hiding is a theme in the Bible. Whatever the cause, the pain, shame, or sense of rejection we experience can undermine the very foundations of our being. Without being firmly grounded, our legs naturally try to find balance by moving in a different direction.

In the case of the slave Hagar, it was the mistreatment at the hands of Sarai, her employer, that caused her to flee. Forced into sleeping with her boss so that the couple would have a child, Hagar understandably got resentful. Tired of serving, tired of sharing herself, tired of being invisible, tired of being expected to throw confetti for something unfair, she headed for the hills. I really don't blame her.

Sarai's cruel treatment of Hagar also is not surprising, since Sarai's heart was in full-blown anguish by now. (After all, *she* wasn't the one who was pregnant, after dreaming of it for decades.) Abram must have felt like he was watching children play an atrocious game of teeter-totter. If you've ever been on the opposite end of someone playing cruel, then you know just how dangerous it is to be the person sitting across from their foul play. With the shame and anger of Sarai on one side and the pain and angst of Hagar on the other, trying to find any balance here was out of the question.

We know it was bad because pregnant Hagar chose to run, not knowing where the next kitchen, bathroom, or bedroom would be! But the light has a way of coming for us. It came for Hagar. God graciously pursued the servant girl because when God wants to reveal Himself, He will, and He will do it in whatever way He chooses. In this account He sent an angel to tell Hagar of encouraging things to come. She responded to the angel's words with wonder, saying, "You are the God who sees me" (Genesis 16:13 NLT).

When *hooray* is extended and an encouraging word is spoken to us, we feel known, seen, and cared for. Confetti can find us anywhere, under any kind of circumstance. If people can't lend their voices to cheer for us, then I believe God will go to great lengths to make sure our hearts have *hooray* through other means. He has a purpose for us, as He did Hagar, and He purposes things inside of us that we are uniquely intended to carry.

Sometimes that can be hard. There are all kinds of people and all kinds of circumstances that will try to dim our light, cause us to get tripped up, and make us want to run or hide. We have to hold our ground, and help others hold their ground as well. Being surrounded as I am by hunters, I think of it this way: we have to be people who can see from a different vantage point, much like a hunting guide who helps shift our lens so our aim can stay on target.

To shine and extend what God has put inside of us, we will have to step out into the open and share ourselves. We need to share ourselves by being seen, being present, and seeing others as we serve them.

CAPES

When our son, Asher, started his first year of preschool, he wore a cape for the first two weeks and told all his new peers that his name was Spider-Man, even though Spider-Man doesn't wear a cape. Asher had them so convinced I started to wonder if he believed himself to actually be Spider-Man.

It was puzzling, though. Once we'd get home from school, he'd lose the cape, drop the act, and get comfortable. After about a week into this new regimen I asked him the obvious question: "Why do you continue to wear your cape to school, honey?" He responded all too quickly, "Because boys don't wear lipstick, Mommy."

Hmm. First of all, he was *four*. Second, I naturally began to want to explore with him this enlightening game of observation about the things we wear to feel okay as we head into the world. I dropped the topic of lipstick, though, and kept watching.

The second week rolled around, and I wondered to my husband if we might need to explore this Spider-Man idea with a counselor. Brian assured me that since his teacher didn't mind a bit, we should let him continue until he tired of it.

He did tire of the cape. When I asked him why he felt ready to let it go, Asher shrugged and said he didn't need it anymore because everyone already knew he was strong and fast.

I realized then that the cape had acted like a covering for him. That makes sense. He was facing a new setting outside his home and outside his comfort zone. The cape gave him a sense of security and made (in his mind) a clear statement about who he was.

We all have capes we throw on for reassurance. As we get older, we become more clever about the kinds of camouflage we use to make us feel secure. Our capes come in a variety of forms and sizes. They might be busyness and productivity. We might fill our lives with relationships and after-school activities, drinking and eating, movies and books, blogs and gyms, rituals, words, and arguments. I for one hated letting go of the things that seemed to "get me through." Shopping and shows certainly didn't seem like numbing or escaping for me until God pulled the curtain back and asked me to "drop the cape" for a bit so He could be my "all consuming." I'd be in a heap of trouble if wine didn't give me such a bad headache.

There are so many things around us with which we can hide, exploit, or momentarily heal ourselves, until we eventually come to the end of ourselves.

To the place where we stop pretending and start presenting who we really are.

If we are going to be an honest voice and expression to others and love them well, it will mean that we need to come out of the places we hide in so that we can lend a hand and join in heaven's applause. At some point we have to retire the cape, remove the facades, and wrap ourselves up in the only stronghold we have permission to dwell in. Our minds must find rest in the fact that regardless of any external factor our souls are loved and accepted, worthy and enough. And so are the souls of others.

WARDROBE

The Apostle Paul makes an outrageous statement in Romans 13:14, where he writes, "Clothe yourself with the presence of the Lord Jesus Christ. And don't let yourself think about ways to indulge your evil desires" (NLT). In another book, Paul tells us to wear "compassion, kindness, humility, gentleness and patience" (Colossians 3:12).

Those may not be things you think about when it comes to your Christian character "wardrobe." I tend to feel more comfortable in things less restrictive. Cloaking myself in Paul's list does not always make me as flexible as I'd like.

If you are to "clothe yourself with the presence of the Lord Jesus" as Paul says, that means you actually have to be in the presence of Jesus! So here are some wardrobe tips.

Before you go through your list of tasks for the day, make some time in the morning to pray and invite His workings to be evident in your life. Rid your "closet," your heart, of items like blame, bitterness, and resentment. These things never look good on you. Put on something new. Add kindness to your approach with people. Let gentleness be the tone you use with others. Make patience your best accessory.

Certainly, getting clothed in Christ won't change the things we are dealing with. But it will change how we deal with them. When we clothe ourselves with His presence overtop of whatever we are wearing, He adds a protective piece to our garment. We can walk in peace instead of worry and be covered in confidence instead of fear or dread. Think of it like a white napkin you would drape around your neck when you eat spaghetti. If things are going to get messy, let's at least do our part to prepare so we can catch a little of what's coming.

If we are going to be good cheerleaders for others, we need to exercise these things in our lives—consistently, energetically, as if we were getting in shape for the next 5K. Otherwise the next person who cuts you off in traffic will bring out your inner toddler, and words you didn't know you still knew will come flying out. Your mess will be on full display, so ask His Holy Spirit for help, guidance, and the placement of His nature to lead you as you surrender to Him.

Trust me, once you are fitted, you will have more to offer someone else. All too often we get into a rhythm of "wake and rush," and when we encounter others, we end up trying to give them something that isn't in our account to begin with. It's no wonder the debt ratio is so high among Americans; we are always in such a hurry.

The goal here is that we need to let the good things cloak us daily, choke us a little if necessary, until we get used to how *hooray* feels on us. Transformation and renewal take time, but if you wear something long enough, people will eventually come to recognize you by it.

I could always see my grandmother's gigantic fake-gold earrings and bright lipstick from the other end of the mall. I have no idea what my kids will say about me; hopefully it has less to do with my physical wardrobe and more to do with my spiritual love— but I'd be just fine with both.

IN HIS PRESENCE

God wants to be a tangible place where we can make trade-offs. In Psalm 91:1 He calls Himself a "shelter." The word in Hebrew means "hiding place." I know we've talked about getting out of hiding, but there is a healthy and proper place to find solace. God offers us His presence as a place to take cover and seek refuge. A place to be consoled, protected, and cared for by His presence.

God's intention is to make Himself so real that when we come to Him, we find actual cover and protection from the things around us. Comfort and peace in Him, that is a place I want to find myself returning to again and again.

This is not found in a building; rather where I can be tucked beneath the arms of a loving Father who hears, heals, speaks, and guides me as I daily wait on Him and walk with Him. I need help on a constant basis, and all I have to do to find it is get quiet and close as I lean in and listen.

HIDING PLACES

There was a great poet and warrior named David who knew how to take proper shelter. In Psalm 17:8 he wrote, "Hide me in the shadow of your wings." Before David got a new title and became King David, he was forced to flee. There was a point in his life, which we can read about in 1 Samuel 24, where David found himself on the run and in need of protection.

Much like the account with Hagar, there was an authority over David that saw him and protected him. David ended up in hiding with a group of warriors inside a cave, concealed from the jealous King Saul who, in a very human detail in the biblical story, needed to take a potty break.

So Saul parked his horse, and wouldn't you know it, the spot he headed to was David's safe place.

> David and his men were far back in the cave. The men said, "This is the day the LORD spoke of when he said to you, 'I will give your enemy into your hands for you to deal with as you wish.'" Then David crept up unnoticed and cut off a corner of Saul's robe. (1 Samuel 24:3-4)

David moved in, but carefully. Not every place to which we go to be concealed will provide us with safe covering. But when we stay sheltered in the right place with a pure heart, as David did, God seems to have a way of dealing with what we've been dealt.

On the other hand, our search for security can lead us into captivity. I imagine the bar, the mall, the computer screen, and other forms of momentary escapes have brought many to seek recovery. I don't think most people formulated a plan to become addicted, but sometimes our safety nets can end up strangling us, so we must be thoughtful about where we go to seek shelter.

For David the cave brought protection, but as Saul tucked in for solace, he only found himself exposed. I'd like to note that our hiding places will do both things simultaneously; they will both protect and expose accordingly.

Where we hide won't always reveal what we are hiding from, but it will bring about exposure. God will expose the things that hinder us from growth and help us heal as we tuck in with Him. The only way to navigate that cave well is with a deep knowing that you are in a safe and treasured place with a good and loving God. In that sense, we can move about freely. For, as Jesus says in Luke 8:17, there is "nothing concealed that will not be known or brought out into the open."

This is a journey each of us will need to take for ourselves. We can watch others walk it, be around people who talk about it, grow up in families that nurture it, but each of us will have to navigate God's shelter for ourselves. For us to truly understand God's good nature, we will have to experience the tangible benefits of walking in the company of the One Who gave us life.

This is incredibly important because though we can still be a voice that lends *hooray* while we are hurting, it will be hard for our words to echo in the ears of others if we remain in the wrong place of hiding. The fact is that people who hide for too long get used to the dark, and their words and actions reflect it.

The words of Isaiah are reverberating in my ears: "Say to the captives, 'Come out,' and to those in darkness, 'Be free!'" (Isaiah 49:9). Let's be actual light to others and help end this long-standing game of hide-and-seek with those who have gotten used to the dark.

.

ARISE & SHINE

Isaiah tells us the first step to ending a standoff is to *come out*. Come out into the light and breathe deeply. Take a step, then the next one, then one more. Bravery is courageous behavior, not a courageous feeling. If you don't feel brave, so what. You don't need to feel it in order to have forward movement.

What are we so afraid of anyway? That we aren't enough? That we don't measure up? That people will see our faults and flaws? We all have them and we all feel that way, so you'll find yourself in the crowd on this one. If being seen is what you're worried about, then you'll blend right in.

People of God don't have the privilege of withholding or holding back from people who need to be helped, loved, or supported. We are called to more than that. We have a mandate to tell, to shine, to share, to say, to believe, to act, and to be. To be light in a dark place. Light to the world, not just a light inside a church.

Plenty of churches are all lit up on Sunday morning, but then where does the light go? Hopefully not into hiding for the week, but back into the world. Plenty of churches can be like a cave too, by the way; it can provide safety and even keep you hidden if it's big enough.

If it starts to feel a little scary, though, as if you're trapped inside a lion's den, then pay attention to those feelings that rise to the surface when you're inside a service. Let's be prayerful about dwelling there for too long. God warns us about wolves that make their homes among sheep, which brings us back to Saul.

INSECURITY

King Saul was picked from all his fellow Israelites, and "there was no one more impressive" (1 Samuel 9:2 csb). He didn't believe it, though, which made any "gifted" person around him a threat.

If the people you surround yourself with always make you feel bigger, then you won't have to worry, much less be able to relate to this problem. However, when you run in a group where people's gifts are evident, their portions are noticeable, and their lights are bright, you will have to decide what you will do with your insecurity.

Insecurity is like bad wiring to our light. It tampers with how well we shine. It hinders the radiance we can bring to others. That's how David ended up in the cave, taking cover from a very insecure king, a king who had everything to gain and nothing to lose by keeping David close to him. The problem with insecurity and its partner, jealousy, is that they seek to protect self, and by doing so forfeit the chance to cheer and spoil the opportunity for the team.

This is the sad story we tell about King Saul. How he chased away the boy who would play the harp for him and who saved the nation by slaying a giant, the man who was best friends with Saul's son Jonathan and husband to Saul's daughter Michal. Think about what a wildly different story we could be telling about King Saul's legacy—had he been a voice of *hooray* and help to the young leader underneath him.

We could be in Bible studies looking at Saul's leadership and his wonderful family dynamics, how his wisdom was so far reaching, his humility unmatched, and his value for team not only commendable but a rare example of how we can run hand in hand with others without pride, arrogance, or insecurity getting in the way.

We don't tell that story, though. His legacy is one of loss. *Hooray* was never extended because his ego was hurt and his insecurity was so off the charts that he chased after David, the lover of God, for more than a decade. He later abandoned his throne because of disobedience, lost his sons in war, and eventually met his death by suicide when he realized he couldn't win.

Insecurity and jealousy leave a bad legacy. How we act now will be remembered, and how we handle those around us will be noticed. Anytime we squelch what God has put inside of someone else, that needs to be addressed. Let's let Saul's path be his own.

BACK TO DAVID

We are saying something with our lives by the way we are living. Our microphones don't have to be held to our lips for people to hear us. The choices we make and the acts of service we extend are loud and clear.

As David had the opportunity in the cave to sneak up on his enemy, his men were pleading with him to end the years of running and take the life of the jealous king. The choice David made sheds light on how we should handle the Sauls in our lives. Here's what he said.

> The LORD forbid that I should do such a thing to my master, the LORD's anointed, or lay my hand on him; for he is the anointed of the LORD. (1 Samuel 24:6)

If you missed it, it's about honor. David gets close to Saul only to show him that he is not a threat. He backs off and puts down the sword. That is how we move forward even with those who can't move with us. We honor them anyway, and we give them room. Not everyone can handle all of who God made you to be. Turn your attention toward the people God does surround you with, and say a prayer for the ones who can't seem to accept your strength. God knows the people who can stand next to us, hold up our arms, and applaud our efforts.

WHAT WILL IT BE?

Can we pause for a second? David called the man who chased him out of town and away from those he loved "delightful."

> Saul and Jonathan, beloved and delightful in life . . .
> they were swifter than eagles, they were mightier than
> lions. (2 Samuel 1:23 NASB)

Not only did David mourn the death of Israel's first king, but he was able to spread confetti on Saul's legacy. David made a choice to honor and cheer for someone who didn't clap for him. Hagar came out of hiding and returned to her mistress to have her baby. We all have choices to make, and each of us will be an expression of those choices. May each of those expressions leave a legacy that helps others shine brighter because of our good choosing.

Meditation

Your embodiment of love and the unique way you express it are a gift to this world. You carry a light that we need. That's why it's so important to make sure you come out of hiding. I promise you that we can handle your fire.

So with that in mind, let's ponder some thoughts:
- Do you find yourself hiding from something/someone right now? If yes, where do you escape?
- Did any emotions surface while you read this last bit on comparison/insecurity/jealousy? How do you deal with these, along with honor, in your own life?

REFLECTION

If I'm finding myself in a place of hiding instead of shining or extending, then I don't just need a good verse to recall, I need a revelation of God's love and a word from Him specifically concerning who I am. God longs to speak to each child He has created. A loving Father wouldn't have it any other way.

Take a minute to get quiet and ask God to say something. Nothing brings change like new clarity concerning who we are and how we were made. In the meantime, tuck this one away.

"Before I shaped you in the womb, I knew all about you. Before you saw the light of day, I had holy plans for you." (Jeremiah 1:5 MSG)

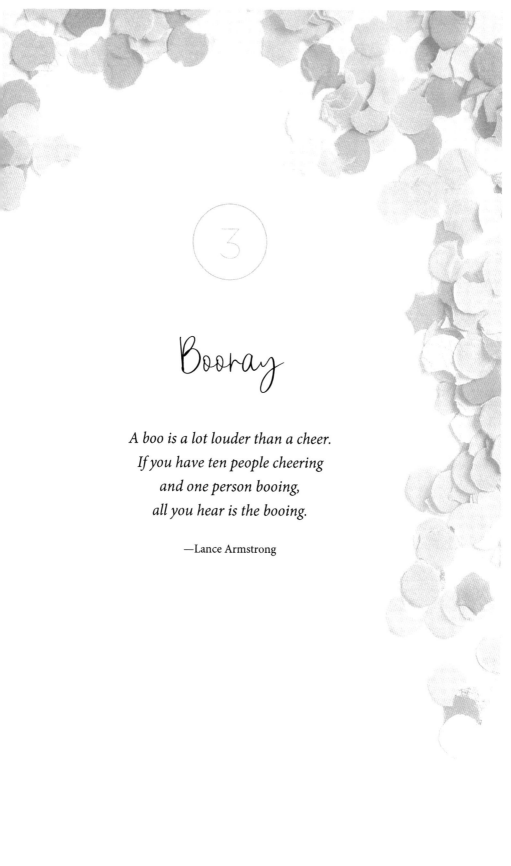

3

Booray

A boo is a lot louder than a cheer.
If you have ten people cheering
and one person booing,
all you hear is the booing.

—Lance Armstrong

THE HEART OF BOO

Brian and I had been married for five months, just out of the honeymoon stage. We were having some pillow talk—no, really, we were just talking—when I made a very *booray* mistake.

I had been thinking of how to give my husband some great ideas on how he could lose some of his recent marital weight gain. I know . . . I'm sinking in my seat as I write this. We had just decided that it would be best to put our financial budget on paper instead of my husband keeping track of it in his head. So, talking about money and all, I should have realized tensions were a little higher than typical.

Then Brian asked, "What do you think we can cut in our budget and not miss too much?"

I saw an immediate opportunity. Without hesitation (you have to imagine my voice dripping with sarcasm) I said, "How about your gym membership?"

That rude little remark led to raised voices, bathroom locking, eye-rolling, and then an eye-opening conversation. I'm not sure what Brené Brown would say about this little incident, but I'm pretty certain it fits into the category of shaming.

I have many stories of being undone by the boos of others. But I could fill a chapter, if not a whole book, with examples of my own *booray* riding shotgun while my *hooray* hides in the back seat. My judgment and my kindness can't sit together. I seem to have a fast tongue when it comes to faults and flaws in others. In other words, the log in my own eye hasn't blinded me yet.

FALLING STARS

By now you probably are catching on that I'm using the term *booray* to describe what I know all of us have experienced, both in the giving and the receiving. *Booray* is when we don't lend our applause; we extend our complaints. It's when we choose to belittle instead of celebrate. We criticize another person's uniqueness. We deliberately "withhold good" from someone when it is within our power to act (see Proverbs 3:27).

Boo is more than having a bad day; it's having a wounded heart. It creates a mess that, if left unattended, spreads like an infection. We each need to get ahold of the cause of our boo. Otherwise we'll pass it on to future generations like bad genes.

Where did *booray* slither onto the scene? You can probably guess. We already saw, when Adam and Eve were out for their walk in Genesis 3, that the snake was on-site without invitation but with plenty to say.

However, the serpent was around long before God breathed life into the first couple. Jesus told His friends that He witnessed Lucifer's descent. "I saw Satan fall like lightning from heaven" (Luke 10:18). If we flip back to Isaiah 14, we can find more history. The once "bright morning star" (CEV) sought to set up his own throne above the stars of God, wanting to make himself *like* the Most High. It didn't work out well for him.

Since then, Satan has had plenty of cohorts to help push his agenda because other angels went dark and followed his lead.

It sounds like a scene straight from Hollywood. The words the Apostle Paul scripted in Ephesians 6:12 read like a preview for us. Only it's not a movie; it's our life.

> Our struggle is not against flesh and blood, but against the rulers, against the authorities, against the powers of this dark world.

The enemy didn't come just to fight with Adam and Eve. He came to battle their offspring. That's us. God said, "I will put hostility between you and the woman, and between your offspring and her offspring. He will strike your head, and you will strike his heel" (Genesis 3:15 CSB).

In other words, war is all around us.

THE REAL ENEMY

The Bible gives the boo-spewing serpent many names, but his character doesn't change. He is crafty, he is sneaky, and he is a liar. Jesus said of the devil, "When he lies, he speaks his native language, for he is a liar and the father of lies" (John 8:44).

His nature is to taunt us with fabrications and falsify the truth with corruption. Any time we start to agree with his slander and accusations, *hooray* comes to a halt in us and the seed for *booray* is planted.

It's very hard to keep the right perspective when we start thinking like the snake. When we choose to match our voice to the voice of "the accuser of our brothers and sisters" (Revelation 12:10), we end up participating in the tearing down of another person our Maker has woven together and thought so carefully about. I've been on the giving and receiving end of boo, and it's downright destructive.

We live in a fallen world, so of course people are going to make us mad, get on our nerves, and hurt our feelings. How we handle our reactions oftentimes is the indicator of how much boo we are dealing with in our own hearts. If we don't recognize and confront our serpent-shaped boo, then we begin to minimize others. Minimization is an overflow of a heart buried in *booray*.

When we wear the same lens as the serpent, we see life as a contest and people as competitors. Everyone always seems bigger when we live life on our belly. (Be gentle when you see people who feel the need to slither. It has to be exhausting living a life with such a skewed lens and dirt in your face, always making moves in secret to get on top.)

Then we often take boo one step further and invite others into our slander by rallying them to agree with us about the irritating things that we are seeing in someone else. We make our *booray* contagious.

Friends, an infected heart needs some help. In the long run the boos you yell at others won't ever build you up on the inside. You have to come against the boo that's causing chaos and give it a name. Is it envy, jealousy, insecurity, hate, anger, pride? How is it manifested? In gossip, drama, arguments, depression, self-sabotage?

Denial gets us nowhere; keeping a busy schedule so that you never have to reflect is a sure way to keep yourself from growth.

When we take inventory of what's plaguing our hearts and depreciating our *hooray*, then we can take it to God and ask for a bigger picture. We can ask Him what He sees and what He wants to say about it.

SANITIZE

Human history was changed in Eden by one conversation, and history is still being changed by conversations. Whether at a dinner table, a conference table, or a communion table, our words have an impact.

Our countless daily exchanges with people may well be influencing how they understand themselves and their lives. Have you ever thought about that? A random comment might raise questions in the other person, like *Do I have what it takes? What is my worth? Is this behavior wrong? Is that decision right?*

That can be innocent enough. But we really must do our best to steward our words well. Otherwise, we might be infected by the snake's tactics. He's been accusing God's children and distorting God's truth for generations upon generations. He's always on the lookout for open ears to whisper into and open palms to twist.

Do you doubt the existence of such an enemy? Just because he's invisible doesn't make him any less real. Think of invisible germs. The war against them is less eternally toxic than the battle against evil. For that matter, think of the huge precautions the world has had to take with the onset of COVID-19. We can't see the virus, but we certainly can see its effects and must be diligent with preventative measures.

I think the same thing needs to be done with our boo. We need to get into the habit of running our thoughts through some mental sanitizer before we offer words that can make someone else sick. Certainly pack a mask if you can't trust your lips.

I've been trying to ask myself three quick sanitizing questions before I extend my words.

- Is this at all beneficial?
- Is this even biblical?
- Is this loving?

This three-part filter would have been great to have had when I was younger, when my only criterion for sifting was "Is this true?" If yes, then I thought I had better bring it up so that the other person could change.

Thankfully, I have friends with extremely strong loyalty genes and sisters excelling in forgiveness. But I can't imagine how many conversations I could have prevented from getting polluted if I would have first sifted my thoughts through some sanitizer.

CONSIDER WHAT YOU HEAR

After Adam and Eve got trapped by boo, God told Adam his curse came because he *listened* to his wife. Once we have listened to an accuser or a false thought, it's likely that we will then move toward action. Human beings act on what they believe to be true. Therefore, we must be careful about which words we are listening to! Maybe that's why Jesus told His disciples, "Consider carefully what you hear" (Mark 4:24).

Sadly, I think it can be easier for us to hang onto the harmful boo words that we hear than the good ones. Most of us don't actually need help from others when it comes to accusing ourselves of things. We're already well acquainted with our own weaknesses, right?

If we already have a bent toward believing the bad—or what we and others believe is bad about ourselves—that can give other people's *booray* a lot of power over us. And cruelty cuts deep. It takes time to let truth mend the wounds.

But dealing with boo thoughts is like deciding whether or not to wear something: it's one thing just to pick it up and examine it; it's another to accept the price and buy it.

SIT DOWN, MARTHA

A woman named Martha opened her home to Jesus and His guys as they were traveling through town. Martha had a sister named Mary. They were definitely different personalities! Mary chose to hang out with the guests—actually, to literally hang on Jesus's every word. Meanwhile, Martha—who I envision as the older one and the type who probably wouldn't even like someone butting in while she cooked anyway—had chosen to "entertain" the famous Rabbi with a big spread. Now she was getting sweaty and was knee-deep in frustration.

So she interrupted Jesus (!). She indirectly but publicly slammed Him for not caring about her being overworked, and she indirectly but publicly slammed Mary for what she saw as irresponsibility and selfishness.

But Jesus wasn't going to accept Martha's double *booray*.

> "Lord, don't you care that my sister has left me to serve alone? So tell her to give me a hand."
>
> The Lord answered her, "Martha, Martha, you are worried and upset about many things, but one thing is necessary. Mary has made the right choice, and it will not be taken away from her." (Luke 10:40-41 CSB)

I don't believe it was a passive-aggressive move that brought Mary to the feet of Jesus. She wasn't trying to get out of something;

she was trying to get something: the Truth. Jesus wasn't gonna make her give that up and go ladle the lentil soup.

I imagine Martha slunk back to the kitchen with her heart heavy and her head low. But those lessons are worth their weight in gold. God gives us insight to help us, not to hurt us, as any good friend would. I doubt that for the rest of her days, Martha ever made the mistake of prioritizing food preparations when she had Jesus, the Bread of Life, in her presence.

By the way, I'd want Martha on my team any day. She'd be an incredible manager. On the other hand, Mary might not have shown very good EQ sense, not being aware of how her choice would impact Martha (at least, as far as we know).

After her chat with JC, Martha might not have been ready for pom-poms yet, but His words helped her to get over her boo. The presence of God can do that for us, always offering us a new perspective.

LOWLY

For *booray* to be banished in us, we have to practice walking in *hooray*. We have to get close to God to be softened by His heart and then listen to His heartbeat for others.

Where do we find Him? In the "humble position of a slave." Remember what the Apostle Paul wrote to the Philippians?

> You must have the same attitude that Christ Jesus had. Though he was God, he did not think of equality with God as something to cling to. Instead, he gave up his divine privileges; he took the humble position of a slave and was born as a human being. When he appeared in human form, he humbled himself in obedience to God and died a criminal's death on a cross. (Philippians 2:5-8 NLT)

God has called us to a position of lowliness, not to be slithering around but to be on the bottom in order to lift others up. If you're not just a little sore, then you might still have some bending to do. God builds things on the backs of those who are willing to follow His example.

The Church was started because Jesus chose to carry our burden with the crushing weight of a cross. Getting low is painful, but it's the only way to get close to God.

If you're ambitious, remember that God exalts who He wants to, at the time that He wants to, by any means He wants. No amount of slithering is going to get you higher sooner.

Some of us need to get to a higher place, have a good brushing off, and position ourselves before God to get clarity from His point of view. He has something good to say to you and something good to say *about* you, so get up to listen. "Come up here, and I will show you . . ." (Revelation 4:1).

THE ANTIDOTE

Thankfully, God has an Rx for our boo. But I have to say, it can be tough medicine.

You may have heard of Joseph and his coat of many colors. It's a long story, involving a dysfunctional family, threats of murder, slavery, deceit, false imprisonment, weird dreams, attempted adultery, unbelievable wealth and power, famine, and, ultimately, faith and the triumph of *hooray*. Hold on to your seats!

Genesis 37 tells us that Joseph was his father's favorite son. As a sign of his favor, Dad (his name was Jacob) gave Joey some very fancy outerwear. The gift didn't do him any favors with his older brothers. But at seventeen, Joseph was pretty clueless about his siblings' feelings for him. They were a rough lot. Cruel and lawless, actually. And jealous.

> When his brothers saw that their father loved [Joseph] more than any of them, they hated him and could not speak a kind word to him. (Genesis 37:4)

Our feelings can stay stuffed down for only so long. Eventually our inner *booray* will burst out, one way or another. If we're wise, we will take a look at it and figure out the cause. Justifying it or denying it only keeps us from healing.

Unfortunately, Joseph's brothers were not interested in self-examination. At the same time, young Joseph was pretty foolish too, virtually taunting them with his coat and with accounts of his dreams that suggested he would eventually rule over them. You can anticipate the trouble that is coming, can't you? But there also is a thread of God's favor woven into the story. Hold on to that thought; it will make sense at the end.

All but one of the brothers wanted to murder Joseph. That's one sign of favor. Instead, the boys stripped him and threw him into a pit. Then they sat down and ate lunch.

Just then, another sign of favor: God sent a caravan on its way to Egypt, full of traders who bought Joseph as a slave for twenty pieces of silver. Then his brothers ripped up his colorful coat, doused it with blood, and took it to Dad, heartlessly making up an elaborate story that young Joey had been torn to pieces by an animal. Now it was Jacob whose heart was torn to pieces. Unchecked, *booray*'s destruction expands exponentially, doesn't it?

Meanwhile, favor followed Joseph despite being enslaved. He was sold to a high-level officer of Pharaoh himself, a guy named Potiphar. Potiphar spotted Joseph's potential and put him in charge of his household. More favor.

> From the time that [Potiphar] put [Joseph] in charge of his household and of all that he owned, the Lord blessed the Egyptian's house because of Joseph. The Lord's blessing was on all that he owned, in his house and in his fields. (Genesis 39:5 CSB).

However, the evil one tried to derail Joseph here, using Potiphar's wife to tempt him into adultery. When Joseph remained a man of honor, she made up an accusation, which landed young Joey in prison. Another pit! Again, though, there was favor. The warden admired Joseph and made him under-warden, and he was able to interpret dreams for two of Pharaoh's former staffers, claiming, "Do not interpretations belong to God?" (Genesis 40:8).

God can use a person like that, one who not only leans on God but also credits Him with the revelation. Still, there was no freedom for Joseph yet. Promotions often come about because of the perseverance we practice while patiently sitting in the pit. How we handle our tests will determine the next move we can make, not the genie wishes that we want God to grant us. Plus, God always has a big picture in mind that we can't see.

Then something big did change. God planted another dream, this time with Pharaoh. Because of Joseph's reputation for accurate dream interpretation, he was summoned from prison, cleaned up, and ordered in front of the most powerful man in Egypt. (Pretty ironic, right? Interpreting a dream got him into the original pit. Now, years later, it would get him out of another one.)

Joseph gave Pharaoh the difficult interpretation of the dream. Seven years of famine were on their way. But God was gracious to provide a strategy as well. It's one thing to know what God is saying; it's another thing to know what to do about what He says. Don't just ask God, "What is this about?" Also ask Him, "What should I do about it?" Thankfully, Pharaoh had a mind to listen to Joseph, and he put him in charge of everything he had.

Fast-forward. Joseph's brothers were suffering from the famine and traveled to Egypt to buy provisions for survival. They were about to meet up with their little brother Joseph, only they didn't know it was him. On Joseph's side, all kinds of emotions set in as he watched his brothers bow before him. His heart must have whispered to God, "This isn't how I thought the dream would play out."

We can't put God into any kind of box, expecting to apply a formula like THIS EVENT *plus* THIS BEHAVIOR *always equals* THIS OUTCOME. But Joseph's story helps us gain insight to how God can work *booray* events out for our good if we are willing to conform our character to Christ's and trust Him through the trials we face.

Joseph faced hardship because of the actions and boos of others, and nothing about that is fair. But God can take a bad circumstance and bring an unlikely outcome by using the trials we face as a means of transportation for us. Trials can be our transportation to get us to the places we are supposed to go.

In the end, God allowed the boos of Joseph's brothers to bring about the promotion that Joey dreamt of as a boy. We need to be able to see a bigger picture when we are in the middle of getting booed. I'm not talking about getting walked on or about not having boundaries with people that hurt us; I'm saying we need the mind of God to expand our thinking about what is currently happening. What we deem as tragedy can be the building blocks God uses to move us into our future.

When Joseph came down to eye level with his brothers, he wasn't demanding justice be done for the tragic way they treated him. He was the one encouraging them because he knew God was telling a bigger story.

Don't be grieved or angry with yourselves for selling me here, because God sent me ahead of you to preserve life. For the famine has been in the land these two years, and there will be five more years . . . God sent me ahead of you to establish you as a remnant within the land and to keep you alive by a great deliverance. Therefore it was not you who sent me here, but God. (Genesis 45:5-8 CSB)

When the boos come our way, leave a little room for a "but God." That does not mean it won't hurt or be hard. But if you want a formula, here is one we can count on.

THE BOOS OF OTHERS *plus* CONFORMITY IN OUR CHARACTER TO CHRIST *equals* AN OPPORTUNITY FOR GOD TO DO SOMETHING BIG.

JUST FLIP IT

So be attentive to what attributes are under attack in your life. Most likely, what the enemy dislikes is something about how God made you that He wants to show off and highlight—an expression that's uniquely yours to offer.

For example, last year my daughter, Ruby, was the only blond, blue-eyed white girl in her class. The school is charming, the teachers are wonderful, but kids are kids no matter how incredible the setting. Ruby was an easy target. The verbal assaults always seemed to tear at the way she is uniquely designed.

Booray doesn't seek to celebrate differences and applaud uniqueness. It has a mindset that seeks to destroy whatever it doesn't understand. But just like a mediocre poker player who has overplayed his hand, *booray* shows its cards early. Whatever is getting pointed out and picked on is the very thing that God wants to show off and elevate.

This means it's not all that difficult to counteract someone's boo when it lands on you. It's a strategy similar to the one I use when I make a pancake. You just need to know when to flip it.

I know it's time to flip my pancakes when the batter starts to bubble up. If I wait too long, I'm gonna have to deal with the aftermath of burnt stuff. When you deal with emotions from boo attacks, or when you notice the emotions of your dear ones starting to bubble up, it's time to flip it so you can see a new side.

So, do some inspecting about whatever seems to be under fire in your life. What is below the surface? Yes, I recognize that it's not as simple as flipping pancakes, but I can promise the payoff is sweeter.

When I sat with my daughter as she started to bubble up about the *booray* thrown at her, I got to speak a new word over her. I thanked God that He can turn anything for good and use what others are pointing their finger at as something He can brag about. Ruby and I celebrated all the wonderful things that make her unique and special. Will that make future assaults hurt less? I doubt it, but the next time someone flings boo at her, a better word has already been planted.

I want to teach Ruby early that only weakness assaults strength. Insecurity wants to hurt anyone in its path so that it can feel stronger. But really, someone else's boo has nothing to do with you.

So keep your head up, darling, and learn to just flip it.

A *BOORAY* PLAGUE

Booray isn't just damaging to individuals. It's a pandemic infecting our whole society on the scale of COVID-19. And because of social media we don't have to be in public places to catch it.

We are losing honor for committed citizens who uphold our right for freedom. Badges are being abused and are abusing others. Our political climate is toxic, with donkeys and elephants bleeding out on both sides. Our schools and workplaces are an overflow of the thoughts and ideas that we give voice to at home. We need to pay attention to the words being exchanged in these sacred places. It's all becoming an echo chamber of accusations.

Grace and truth were meant to hold hands and swing in harmony. Too many people are getting kicked in the face because we aren't seeking a healthy rhythm out on our playgrounds or in grocery-store aisles. We've forgotten that even if we disagree, we can still choose to honor the other person, no matter where they seem to be standing.

And what about within the Church? We might actually have a pharisaical problem. Remember in Jesus's day, the religious elite could quote chapter and verse. Yet they were blind to the Son of God Who walked among them. He called them "whitewashed tombs" (see Matthew 23:27). Today, our hands may be raised high and our lips may be giving thanks, but love seems only for those who agree with us. We don't know how to applaud people we disagree with "according to the gospel," so we end up hurting them, if not hating them.

That's not how God wants us to show His love to a broken world.

Meditation

God's words are purposed. What if for the entire day you let your words be thoughtfully purposed? What I mean is, focused on saying true and honest things, pleasant and encouraging things.

Let's partner corrective words with kindness and true words with humility. When your boo rises to the surface, let's look to see why it's happening. Let's vow to pick the beautiful words over the void and harmful ones. Let's steward our mouths well with words that will help and heal, and choose carefully what we are saying before we start extending. Let's make it our daily prayer to ask God to show us what He sees in others. When we see what He sees, let's say what He says—and no doubt someone next to you needs that kind word today.

So with that in mind, let's ponder on this question:
- Would you take some time today and pray to hear a word for someone?

REFLECTION

"May these words of my mouth and this meditation of my heart be pleasing in your sight." (Psalm 19:14)

"These are the words in my mouth; these are what I chew on and pray. Accept them when I place them on the morning altar, O God." (Psalm 19:14 MSG)

The Giant of Smallness

*Refuse to be average.
Let your heart soar
as high as it will.*

—A. W. Tozer

DISTORTED IMAGES

I was at a summer fair with my kids when we rushed past one of those crazy mirrors that reflects back to you a wacky, warped image of yourself. What I saw made me halt the troops.

"Hold up!" I ordered. "That can't be right." I was five inches shorter and a foot wider.

It took some convincing to get the kids to do a one-eighty because they had their sights set on the barf coaster. Once they conceded, though, we all stood shoulder to shoulder, face forward, and stared at the contorted versions of ourselves produced by the ludicrous contraption. We laughed and pointed and did little dances and laughed some more. Then we hurried away, making room for the next family to be appalled.

I still think about that distorted mirror. The experience made me realize that sometimes, when we walk into certain places, we don't actually stay our real size. I'd better explain.

WHAT'S YOUR SIZE?

It's easy to shrink or get bent out of shape when whatever we are looking at seems too big, too hard, or too foreign for us to deal with. On top of that, the wrong mirrors will distort our view. That makes all the more reason to know your true size. That's the starting point for empowering you to serve God.

After all, we don't tell "God stories" about people who stay back and choose not to conquer. Risk is always required when we move into new territory. Courage is always part of believing God's promises. Staying your real size means being confident in God's character.

What do I mean by "size"? It's simple. It's knowing what God says about who you are. It's understanding the gifts and abilities He has given you. It's being grounded in God's truth and measured by our faith. And here's another cool thing: our size is constantly growing.

To be able to extend confetti to others, we have to be a people who know how to see past the way things seem in order to embrace a truer reality. Maybe the odds don't look to be in our favor. Maybe there seems no possible way we could do that thing, go to that place, get that job, or [fill in the blank with any thousand different challenges!]. But if we are walking with God, we are walking with the source of power, wisdom, and creativity that can fill any gap!

Think about the great stories you've heard, or lived, in which something happened that looked impossible. Those stories only occur if the people in them know their size, choose to stay their size, decide not to shrink, and trust God enough to step out.

By the way, God's Word is the best mirror you can gaze in, especially if you're experiencing a contorted reality. It will shed light on and reveal your belief system. Our beliefs often determine our perception of our size. The Bible will point to what's true and to what God has promised us.

God's promises and God's truth are like two legs to stand on. You'll need them in order to stay your size, as the Israelites discovered on the borders of the Promised Land.

WHAT DO YOU SEE?

The lens we look through affects what we see. What we see affects what we say and believe. If our lens is *hooray*—if we view things from the perspective of God's promises—then our words will line up with truth and we'll have two strong legs to stand on. But there's always the potential of encountering the warped mirrors of life.

There is a great passage in Numbers 13 that illustrates this. You probably have heard about or read the account of the twelve scouts God told Moses to send into Canaan, which He already had promised Moses that He was going to give to the Israelites. God had confetti ready for His people, but He was testing their hearts before He threw it.

Moses hand-chose these guys. They were the top leader from each tribe. The best of the best. They were all God's people, and they all knew what He had promised—that He was going to give the Israelites the land.

Moses ordered the twelve to explore the region, to see how many people there were and if they were weak or strong, to check if there were fortifications, and to judge if the soil was fertile. And he told them to bring back some fruit. That was one thing they did well. It took two men to carry it all.

Identifying possibilities and problems when undertaking something new is important. Getting intelligence on potential adversaries is crucial. Exploring what you're getting into is wise. But you have to keep focused; otherwise, circumstances can distort your thinking.

That's what happened with these twelve spies, for all but two of them. They spent forty days sneaking around Canaan, and their vision became distorted by fear. Their faith in God vanished. And their conclusion wildly affected what they told Moses and the people when they returned. How we see doesn't only affect what we say, but also how we stand. And that affects everyone around us.

> We went into the land to which you sent us, and it does flow with milk and honey! Here is its fruit. But the people who live there are powerful, and the cities are fortified and very large. (Numbers 13:27-28)

And besides that, they saw what they interpreted as giants, who "were so big that we felt as small as grasshoppers" (Numbers 13:33 CEV).

How these men saw themselves—as "grasshoppers" rather than mighty warriors of God—produced a warped perception, which led to a bad report, which in turn turned everyone away from God's promises, from God Himself.

To consistently voice *hooray* means that we have to have faith in God's promises. For us to stay in faith for those promises means that we have to hold on to what God is saying. Confetti can't fall if we only focus on the distorted things we see and not on what God has said.

REPORTS

All twelve of the scouts saw the giants in Canaan. Ten were scared, and two were not. Those two men viewed the situation through eyes of faith and brought back a good report.

One, Caleb, stood in front of the entire gathering of Israelites and ordered them to shut up and listen! "We should go up and take possession of the land, for we can certainly do it," he said (Numbers 13:30).

Immediately, the ten chosen scaredy-cats shouted Caleb down.

> "We can't attack those people; they are stronger than we are." And they spread among the Israelites a bad report about the land they had explored. They said, "The land we explored devours those living in it. All the people we saw there are of great size." (Numbers 13:31-32)

In some ways, it's understandable. Who hasn't gotten scared by what seemed like a giant? Sometimes we think we are standing tall and doing just fine. Then someone or something appears in our lives that looks bigger, more capable, better suited, even threatening, and we start shrinking.

However, if we can view things as the two courageous men did— through the eyes of faith—we can be a voice of hope and offer *hooray*, even if we're in the minority. What would have happened if five men, or four men, or even three men, had believed

God and brought back a positive report? When fear is the loudest voice in the room, people always lose.

Sometimes victory is determined by a simple numbers game. How we show up and influence others matters.

SYNCING & SINKING

Hooray can't help anyone if those of us who are supposed to be offering it don't speak up. But sometimes our *hooray*, the truth we need to share, doesn't make for happy reactions. In fact, sometimes our words can make people really uncomfortable.

Has extending hope and speaking truth ever gotten you in bad standing with others? Were you in the minority? Did you need to be brave? If we are seeing as God sees and saying what He says, then sharing His *hooray* comes with some risk.

I hope it's not the sort of risk that Caleb and his fellow faithful spy, Joshua, faced though!

Not only did their community refuse to listen to their minority report, the text says the assembled Israelites talked together about how to kill the two of them (see Numbers 14:10)! When others are seeing small, sometimes faith can appear like a loaded weapon, threatening them and the way they see life. They become defensive, or worse. You can get caught in the emotional crossfire.

Hooray can't only be for those with whom we see eye to eye on everything. If we can't agree in a situation, then at a minimum we must be both kind and careful in our observations and dis-agreements, and not move toward disapproval of a person. We don't need to further distort reality with sin. Our hearts are big enough to hold room for love while we differ in opinion.

But it is also important that we, like Caleb and Joshua, do not stand aside passively and neglect to speak up when God calls us to. That is allowing the majority to lead the crowd astray. And if the majority view is wrong, the majority may end up initially winning—and ultimately losing.

In Caleb and Joshua's day, syncing with the crowd got a lot of people in trouble. God punished the ten unfaithful scouts with a plague. The majority of all the adult Israelites were forbidden to step foot in the Promised Land, and they died at its border.

How many of us find ourselves being swayed by fear and getting caught up with the majority, refusing to listen to the voice of the minority? We all face fears: fear of people, fear of rejection, fear of failure, fear of the unknown, fear of all kinds of things that warped mirrors distort and exaggerate.

All twelve of the spies in Canaan could see giants; that was a truth. But ten saw giants and then viewed themselves *by comparison* as grasshoppers. They began to shrink. Meanwhile, the remaining men saw evidence of another truth at hand: the truth that mattered.

Caleb and Joshua made it into the land that God wanted to give His people because they could decipher the difference between *what something seemed like* and *what God said it was going to be like.* That's the hard part about taking ground, moving forward, and helping others step into something. It's not easy. I'm afraid we have become a people accustomed to doing everything the easy way. (Says the girl who just made her "grocery run" with the click of a button.)

What we are seeing has to be weighed by what God is saying. His Word doesn't change. That's hard to swallow sometimes. But if God has said it, then hold on tight to it. His words are like an anchor for us. They act like a deep-settling weight that holds us in place, when others—or the entire world for that matter—seem to be pulling in contrary directions. His whispers can secure our feelings and ground our emotions. If we have not stood with both legs (truth and promises), if we have not planted our feet on the Rock, we will find ourselves syncing with what the crowd is saying. So protect the precious words He whispers in your direction, because those promises will be what protect you.

Holding fast to God's truth even when we're looking at another truth is the embodiment of *hooray*.

EYES TO SEE

I'm reminded of another duo who, much like Caleb and Joshua, matched their voices to God's despite being in the minority.

Mary and Joseph had come to the temple, bringing their newborn baby to be dedicated to the Lord as required by Jewish law. I don't know the number of people who were there that day; there must have been a crowd, maybe hundreds. But only Simeon and Anna had eyes to see the tiny infant Jesus for the godly giant He was going to be.

Simeon, on whom the Holy Spirit rested (see Luke 2:25), and Anna, a very old prophetess from the tribe of Asher (see Luke 2:36), had some astounding things to speak over the nondescript baby held by peasant parents. Thank goodness they spoke up and didn't hold back.

Simeon declared on the spot that his eyes had "seen your salvation . . . a light for revelation to the Gentiles, and the glory of your people Israel" (Luke 2:30, 32). Anna turned into an evangelist. "She . . . spoke about the child to all who were looking forward to the redemption of Jerusalem" (Luke 2:38).

It is one thing for the men and women who traveled with the adult Jesus to recognize Him as the One sent from God. They could watch Him teach and reveal hidden wisdom; they saw the miracles He did. But Simeon and Anna had eyes to see who Jesus was going to be.

People who can see what's not yet, before things are built and before people ever do anything meaningful, are rare gifts. Don't discount the minority. Sometimes they can see the things our hearts haven't adjusted to yet. Find some people in this season of your life who can see what can be, people who don't shrink, people who might even be considered the minority, and I'll bet you'll slay plenty of giants together.

FACING YOUR GOLIATHS

There is another story in the Bible about a giant, a minority, and people who saw things too small.

The scene opens in 1 Samuel 17 with King Saul and the Israelites behind battle lines facing the army of the Philistines. Day after day, they were being taunted by the Philistines' nine-foot champion named Goliath, who yelled insults and threats and challenged them to send out one man for him to fight. Goliath's words and presence made all of Israel shrink in fear.

That was a savvy tactic, one that has echoes in our current culture. Every day, we're taunted by the noisy giants of social media and entertainment, causing us anxiety and fear.

Goliath was doing what bad-guy giants do best, namely playing a game of comparison and relying on their "bigness." Remember, people usually yell because they need validation.

> Goliath stood and shouted to the ranks of Israel, "Why do you come out and line up for battle? Am I not a Philistine, and are you not the servants of Saul?" (1 Samuel 17:8)

First, he taunted them to get them to look at the battle line, a measuring line, because he wanted them to see how far short they were in relation to him. Enemies will do that; they will try to get you to measure yourself by what you see. Never head for a line that will only show you what something *seems* like. That's small thinking.

Also remember that our enemies can say true things, but it's not the Truth. Goliath could have stated the fact that David was smaller and weaker. That was true. But the bigger Truth was that God had gifted and called him. After all, Samuel had anointed David and God's Spirit came upon him powerfully (see 1 Samuel 16:13). David would have all the resources he needed to accomplish God's goals. Can you see how that applies to your own life?

Second, Goliath called them "servants of Saul." That was partially correct. But more importantly, they were servants of God, even if they didn't identify as such (which left them feeling powerless).

Meanwhile, an old man named Jesse was sending his youngest boy, a shepherd named David, on an errand to take some groceries to his big brothers out on the battlefield.

When David rolled up with the grub, he had a couple of advantages. One, he wasn't on the line with the others where measurements were being made, so he wasn't about to make comparisons and feel dismayed. Two, he didn't identify as a servant of a man but of God. When you do that, your resources are endless.

The next scene took a new turn, because Goliath now had a different listener. What we hear can cause our faith to stir or our fear to rise, based on our belief system and how well anchored we are. David, being very grounded, heard the same taunts as the soldiers around him. However, he wasn't going to tolerate them. The giant's words were incongruent with what David knew of Truth. That's why he had confidence to respond the way he did.

> Who is this uncircumcised Philistine that he should defy the armies of the living God? (1 Samuel 17:26)

He didn't say, "Who is defying Saul?" or "Who is defying our nation?" or "Who is defying our morals?" He knew that everything
is under God and rests with God. No matter what a giant said,
David would not be tripped up, and he kept pushing the idea that
someone should do something.

It's interesting that David got yelled at by his oldest brother.
That's not surprising. Sometimes families don't know what God
puts inside of us. The familiar can be a barrier to experiencing
the miraculous if we're not careful.

David was taken to King Saul, to whom he boldly said, "Let no
one lose heart on account of this Philistine; your servant will go
and fight him" (1 Samuel 17:32). Saul basically laughed and told
him "no way." He said David was much too small. Interestingly,
Saul must have been measuring his chances for victory. None of
his warriors had volunteered to confront Goliath, and understandably so. The deal was, if a challenger lost, the Israelites would
become slaves of the Philistines. The human stakes were high.

We can't always wait for our leaders' approval before we step
into things, nor can we be swayed by their opinions of us. There
is more to people than can be seen. David eventually was going
to be Saul's successor (see 1 Samuel 16:12-13), and there wasn't a
man on the field or at home who knew how capable he was. God
validates us, God anoints us, and God puts us in the places that
He sees as fitting for us even when others can't see it.

TRAINING GROUND

Some backstory here. It's good to be reminded that even divinely chosen royal rulers need time to develop. While no one was watching, God had been training David for years to be ready to take on a giant.

To protect his sheep David had fought large and terrifying challengers way before he showed up at King Saul's war. (Read 1 Samuel 17:34-37 for David's own account of his escapades.) That doesn't mean the first time David saw a bear, it wasn't scary to step into that fight. I don't think things always get less scary for us; we just get more accustomed to facing them.

Usually the things we have faced and defeated are a training ground for what's coming next. Thankfully God lets us work things out and win private wars so that when He asks us to step into public places (as He will), we feel equipped and ready—or at least called to the challenge, as David was. Remember, at the right moment, the Prophet Samuel was sent by God to find David and anoint him as the next king. First Samuel 16:13 says that "from that day on the Spirit of the Lord came powerfully upon David."

Now the Lord was about to put David's skills and confidence and faith on public display. David had to push past some mockery (i.e., his jealous brothers, and Saul labeling him "only a boy" [1 Samuel 17:28, 33 cev]). Then Saul tried to weigh him down with his way of doing things. It's one thing to listen to advice from people who are facing war right next to us. It's another to heed instruction from someone who's only willing to watch the war from the castle.

David declined the top-notch armor and walked confidently in his own style, knowing just what it would take for him to win. We can see one lesson from this: as new leaders emerge, let's give them room for some unconventional ways of doing things. Different and unorthodox aren't enemies to defeating giants and winning wars. I wouldn't have thought to put my head down and gather stones while the giant yelled and screamed, but I'll think twice about how I go about my problem-solving the next time I feel intimidated by something. Sometimes the route we take won't make sense to people, but God knows how to use who we are to get us to where we need to be in order to help the ones who need it.

Every giant has a weakness, and David found Goliath's. David walked to the line and sent a rock flying high, landing it right between the giant's eyes. Down Goliath fell because, as big as he was, his seeing was small, and as small as David was, his seeing was large.

STAY YOUR SIZE

If David had shrunk or given up next to Goliath's strength, as did all the other men in the story, world history would have gone a different direction. An entire nation was saved because one person chose to step forward and stay their God-given size.

Like David, we can be out running groceries to family members. Or maybe we're grabbing a coffee with a friend or attending a dinner party. Then something happens, and we have to make a choice. Are we going to follow the crowd and shrink, allowing the giant in the picture to appear tall and loud?

Let me illustrate. I went to pick up my son, Asher, from school for a dentist appointment. When I got there, his class happened to be outside for gym. They were running races.

Prior to attending this school, Asher had been proud to be one of the fastest kids in first grade. However, in his current class, there were plenty of quick-footed boys.

I walked to the fence and watched the children run. Little by little several boys inched their way to the front, but not Asher. Then, as the pack got close to where they would turn for the last leg of the race, I saw my son start walking.

Walking in a race? That sentence didn't make any sense. Maybe if Asher was hurt somehow, but that wasn't the case. So I started yelling. "Run, Asher! Run! Run!"

Heads turned in my direction, people wondering what all the fuss was about. I saw the fretted look on his gym teacher's face.

I had no time to explain that I couldn't care less who came in first or second or last in this race. What I did care about was my son, because I knew what was happening.

I knew Asher loved to run and run fast. But when he was next to someone else's strength, he didn't feel strong or fast, so he let himself shrink. He not only got small, he gave up.

No matter how crazy I sounded, I was not going to be silent while I watched with tears in my eyes as my boy grew small. At the end of the race, his teacher directed him toward me. I was thankful we had a ninety-minute drive. (We live in a semi-rural area.)

Asher eventually recognized that someone else's speed did not motivate him to run faster; it made him give up. What I wanted him to understand was that winning was not the goal—remaining was. We are always going to be taller, smaller, prettier, smarter, faster, or stronger than some. And some are always going to be taller, smaller, prettier, smarter, faster, or stronger than us. So what? It's a win when we can hold our own, be ourselves, and offer what we have even when others next to us might be offering more.

The experience made me reassess how I'm throwing confetti for my kids. Children can start to feel small at a young age. If the parents and adults around them are not careful, our little ones can grow up in performance-based homes if our messages about strength, growth, and courage aren't wrapped in love and acceptance—no matter the outcome. When people can just remain no matter who they're next to, it's worth our applause.

We all have gifts and talents that we need to develop, but we are not loved and valued based on what those things are or how we measure up because of them. If we think we've won because we stand a little taller when we're next to others, we've already lost.

WHEN BEING SMALL BECOMES A BIG PROBLEM

People who tend to feel small generally do one of two things: hide or inflate.

By hiding I mean this: it's when people play small, dumb down, pull back, and conceal what they have to offer. They keep *hooray* to themselves and can't give voice or acknowledgment to any kind of strength in the room. They tuck inside themselves instead of moving close to others. They hide instead of shine. We've been over this, right?

Inflating is so contradictory. We might label as conceited those people who try to prove how gifted they are by "showing off"; maybe we decide that they shouldn't be shown any confetti. But we might be misinterpreting their behavior. There's a good chance they're using the tactic because they feel too small. To feel more accomplished and powerful, they puff themselves up—like an actual puffer fish. In defense mode, when it feels threatened, it will puff itself up, even to the point of literally blowing itself up!

This tactic can move quickly from puffing to stinging. People with this self-belief often put others down because when others are lower, that must mean they are higher. When someone puts others down, we think they are demeaning or even cruel. I believe it's more likely a manifestation of someone who desperately needs affirmation or just simple acknowledgment, proof that someone sees them and they have something good to give.

Strength doesn't point to weakness, though; that's cowardice. Strength is able to offer and to be; to be a presence in a room next to others without fearing, comparing, or concealing. Strength can just be all and every bit of who we were created and meant to be.

Strength doesn't become strong by being better than someone else. Strength doesn't *do*—it just *is*. Strength is at rest because it is someone else's, or rather *we are* Someone else's. We have a royal inheritance as Christ followers, so our supply of the things we need will not run out. That is how you sit and stand and run and be next to other people with tremendous talent, giftedness, and grace over their life. You settle into you by sitting close to God and letting the words He speaks and the love He has become your everything. When your heart is full, you overflow.

When we can know His heart for us and for others, small people aren't our problem. Actually, any kind of people shouldn't be our problem because we can extend good words and give our love as an overflow of His grace. We can be a tangible expression of His kindness and goodness to others. We can release the weight of expectation we place on people, and we can forgive and apologize quickly for any mistakes that may have happened because strength knows how to bow down and go low. Strength doesn't always stand on a pedestal or hold people to unrealistic heights. Strength finds its substance in the presence of God, and where He is present, there is freedom.

The essence of *hooray* has to start with Him. If we're not wrapped up in Him, it will be hard for us to hold ourselves to our size in any room. If we can't be ourselves, then how can we offer ourselves?

IT'S THEIR PROBLEM

Have you ever walked into some place and then excused yourself to the ladies' room to check for BO because people seemed to be giving you noticeable distance?

Friend, here's what you need to know. While I'm not discounting the value of deodorant, the main point is, we aren't the cause of someone else's smallness. In fact, anyone in that state of mind needs you to model how to recognize and stay your God-given size.

So while you're in the bathroom, take a good look in the mirror and adjust your crown. Then walk back to the crowd, because you are needed.

People who see themselves as small may be intimidated by your strength and beauty. They need to get that worked out. You can't get smaller so that they feel bigger. That's inauthentic, and it doesn't help anyone. In fact, if you hold back and help them stay the size they (erroneously) think they are, you're letting them perceive their shaky ground as fit for them to stand on.

No, you stand as a King's kid—at any age—and people need to see you as you are. So carry on, with whatever talent and calling God has given you. I'm not advocating for a show-and-tell with every person we come in contact with. Nor am I implying that flaunting is an admirable trait. I'm just saying that when we walk into a room, we must remain who we are, regardless of what the room is telling us.

JUST REMAIN

A very close friend of Jesus tells us that it's almost impossible to *remain* (i.e., stay faithful) unless we are *abiding*. The Apostle John makes it very clear that unless we are connected to the vine (Jesus), we will run out of life-giving resources.

Other synonyms of *abiding* are *dwelling, enduring,* and *encamping.* The way to strength is by remaining in Him, in front of Him, beside Him, and before Him.

In order to shine, we must be a reflection of something, and we will reflect that which we stand near. Sometimes we're in places that feel too big or uncertain or scary. The way to stay standing in those places is by tucking in close to Him.

When Gabriel, one of the most prominent angelic servants of God, was asked the question "How can I know that what you say is true?" (Luke 1:18 NCV), what was his answer? The archangel could have said plenty about his strengths, his job description, his impressive assignments, or all the things he'd seen and done. Instead the answer he gave for his credentials was based on where he stood.

> I stand in the presence of God, and I have been sent to speak to you. (Luke 1:19)

What credentials do we have that we don't owe to our Maker? What bragging rights can be ours that He hasn't endowed us with?

We don't stand confidently in rooms or with others because of what we carry but because of Who we are trusting to carry us. Our remaining gives us the kind of confidence that makes others the beneficiaries of our standing, and there can be no shrinking when that happens.

Meditation

It can be easy to shrink next to the giants in our lives if we are looking through a lens of comparison. It's best if we just look at those things for what they are and then see what God has to say.

So with that in mind, let's ponder some thoughts:
- Is there something in your life that has you growing small?
- What might God be saying about that?

REFLECTION

Sometimes it's just a small shift, an intentional thought, or a simple reminder that helps us grow up just a little more into who we are. The words of King David and the Apostle Peter are helpful.

The LORD is my shepherd, I lack nothing. (Psalm 23:1)

But you are a chosen race, a royal priesthood, a holy nation, a people for his own possession, that you may proclaim the excellencies of him who called you out of darkness into his marvelous light. (1 Peter 2:9 ESV)

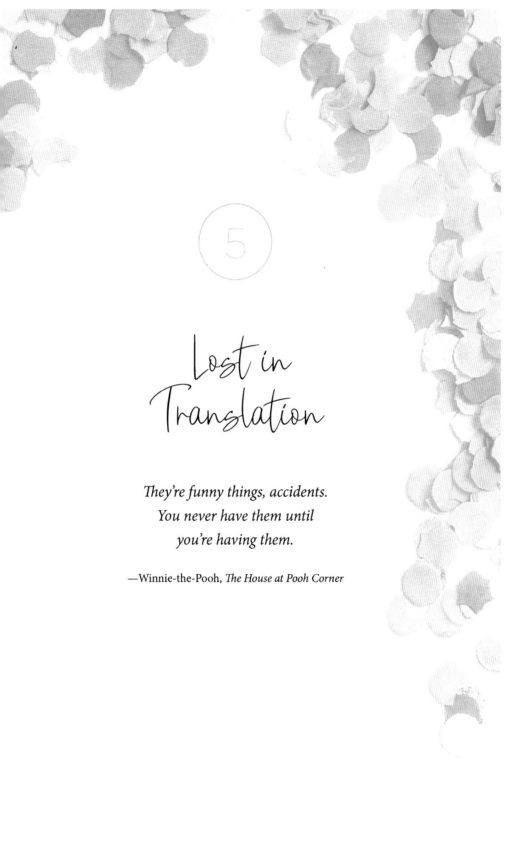

5

Lost in Translation

They're funny things, accidents.
You never have them until
you're having them.

—Winnie-the-Pooh, *The House at Pooh Corner*

BACKSEAT DRIVING

My mother once told me a story of how she and a friend, at age nine or ten, snuck into my grandfather's car and pretended to drive. That wasn't the memorable part, though. As soon as they slid onto the old bench front seat, they proceeded to pull down their pants and underwear! Naturally, I had to ask Mom why on earth they would ever want to pretend to drive Grandpa's car with their little fannies on the cold leather!

She laughed as she explained. "On trips I'd often hear Dad tell Mom to stop 'bare-seat driving.' So we decided we needed to try it out! However, I got the words—and the location—wrong. He was saying, 'Stop *backseat* driving'!"

Things can get messed up in translation, can't they? Lots can get lost in conversations.

Sometimes it's as simple (and funny) as Mom's childish misunderstanding. I think of my darling niece Tilli, who at four years old got increasingly nervous watching the service in which her older brother was getting baptized. She was hearing the pastor say words like *death* and *dying* under "the waters of baptism," and she began to squirm. When we asked her what was wrong, she announced she didn't want her brother to die that day. "I do love him even though I get mad at him," she whispered.

Sometimes it's not so simple. We all have filters when it comes to communication. We run the messages we hear through the lenses of our background, our experiences, our personal biases, and our maturity and education levels (or the gaps in them). If I'm having a bad day, I might start interpreting the tone of my husband's text messages all wrong. I'll be like, "What do you mean, what do I want for dinner?"

That real-life example also illustrates the flip side, when we think we clearly say something to others, and it gets mistranslated and sows confusion. You mean one thing, and your recipient hears something else. It's like a bad version of "Telephone," that old party game we used to play as children. You'd whisper to your neighbor, "Pat the person next to you," and the last kid in the circle would yell, "Pay the price at the toll!"

It's especially painful when we're trying to extend some kindness, and it ends up sounding like correction. I know because I've done it plenty. Confetti doesn't feel good if others are reading you wrong. We need to look at things from all sides and angles to make sure hearts are hearing what we are intending before communication becomes commotion.

It's wise to stop and consider how we're coming across. How are others experiencing you? Your mate, your kids, your family, your friends and coworkers, what's it like for them to be on the other side of you?

Aaack, I sometimes just wish that people could read my mind. I've been married for almost twenty years, and trust me when I tell you that I've given Brian plenty of opportunity to practice through the years, and we still haven't nailed it yet.

HOW IT HAPPENS

Are you like this too? I generally tend to think I am being crystal clear about a situation. Then a lost-in-translation moment happens, and wham, I hate to say it, but I'm shocked.

I was at a nail salon getting a pedicure. The sweet gal working on my feet asked me in a very heavy Korean accent if I needed my nails done too. I said, "Sure, I'd just like to have the old polish taken off and a clear coat put on." When another manicurist, whose first language also was not English, came to my station with a cart full of tools and supplies, like a drill and a powder of some sort, I didn't think anything of it. I just assumed all this equipment must be a new technique for removing polish and prepping me for a quick coat of polish. In my head I knew I had communicated my wishes.

Thirty minutes later I looked down at my new mani. My nails had never looked so good. The technician then asked how often I wanted my acrylics to be changed. Ahh. No wonder they looked fabulous. I had said one thing, but the salon workers had heard another—and I hadn't paid attention because I was certain I had been, uh, clear.

When a misinterpretation takes place due to a communication failure on my part or an assumption made by the other person, I am almost always caught off guard. In this laughable case, the only fallout was the forty dollars I hadn't planned to pay. There have been plenty of other conversational situations that have cost me much more due to the mishap caused by what was being said.

When things get lost or dropped in conversation and we aren't speaking the same language, it can cost us.

I recently had a dream about a friend, which provided me what I thought was some insight she would like to hear. When we got together, I summarized it for her, keeping it short and simple because I figured the message would be obvious. I felt we were on the same page and she'd be tracking. I'll just say thank goodness my friend is a kind person. She had not been tracking at all, and she was not happy about the new revelation I thought would be life-changing for her. She led with grace as we discussed how I might better communicate next time.

Here I thought I was extending a gift, offering confetti, when in fact what actually landed for her was much heavier and caused commotion in her heart. Not ideal.

Think of that word: *commotion*. It means a noisy disturbance. Look at it and see that it's just a few letters off from the word *communication*. Notice something else. The five letters that *commotion* doesn't share with *communication* are "unica," rather similar to the word *unique*.

That makes sense. Each of us is so unique. As we've said, our filters are unique to us. On top of that, no one is perfect. We've got to give each other room when our communication turns into the commotion we didn't intend.

CONTEXT

When I'm feeling rushed or nervous, I can end up being short with others, assuming they can fill in the blanks. Sometimes I'm just tired, and I don't go the extra mile to explain where my comment or observation came from. That can end up wreaking havoc on a heart that needs more at the moment.

I've been on the receiving end of these sorts of missed-message experiences too. The mental gymnastics when trying to pick up the pieces of what's just been said can be exhausting.

Getting lost in translation is much different from *booray,* by the way. Think of it as an issue of a misstep, or misinterpretation, rather than an outward or obvious expression by someone who is clearly not a fan or who makes the choice to withhold and not cheer for you.

Missteps aren't about minimizing someone. They are more about taking a swing and not connecting. Striking out. Painful and awkward, but not malicious.

Not everyone is going to get it when we make an intentional effort in our cheer or move toward change. It's best if we realize that ahead of time; offense is a good strategy.

MISHAP & MISINTERPRETATION

There is a fantastic example in the Bible about a major communication mishap caused by misinterpretation, and by a priest, no less. Not only that, it involves a godly woman whose heart was hurting badly.

The scene is set up like this: A man named Elkanah had two wives. (Here we go!) One of them, Peninnah, had lots of kids—a very big deal in that culture. The other, Hannah, had none. She sure wanted them, though. Every year the whole family would make a trip to a holy place, called Shiloh, where they'd make offerings and worship. And every year, Peni would provoke Hannah until the tears came. Sister wives or not, the Bible makes it clear that these two women were nothing short of rivals.

We pick up the story in 1 Samuel 1:10, where the text tells us that they had just finished up with dinner, all but Hannah. Who could eat while feeling such anguish, and in the midst of such awful company, right? Hannah was standing, apparently in a public spot near the temple. She began to pray silently, her lips moving but no words audible. Turns out she was making a vow. If God would give her a son, she would dedicate him to the Lord. A priest named Eli was nearby, watching and jumping to the wrong conclusion.

> As she kept on praying to the LORD, Eli observed her mouth. Hannah was praying in her heart, and her lips were moving but her voice was not heard. Eli thought she was drunk and said to her, "How long are you going to stay drunk? Put away your wine." (1 Samuel 1:12-14)

Have you ever been there, by the way? When there is nothing coming out of your mouth, only silent murmurs full of ache, layered in pain? No doubt our sighing makes its way to the ears of our God. But it's hard to sit tight while we wait for Him to do something.

I've been through seasons in life when I've had to tuck the Bible in next to me at night and sleep with it like a security blanket while the murmuring was on my lips and the ache moved about in my heart. Sometimes we come out of those seasons with our bellies full of promise. Sometimes we are simply made aware of His tangible presence as we sit in our pain.

Grief is sacred, and it's not a great time for an audience. Eli was observing a private moment without putting on a lens of grace. He had no context about the things Hannah had been through. Therefore he misinterpreted desperation for drunkenness. Sometimes they're related, but not in this case.

Eli had a perfect opportunity to be *hooray* for Hannah by using his voice to extend hope. Instead, his lack of information gave Hannah more pain. He dug into her wound by deeming her drunk and wicked. Yikes, barren and abused, and now the one who speaks for God is doing the name-calling. Hannah had been dealt a bad hand.

It is so hard to respond with grace when others have no context about your situation but think it's fitting to offer advice anyway. I for one hate being misunderstood, and I can't say that tenderness is the emotion that rises when someone is coming at me sideways. I think that's why I am flabbergasted when I read how Hannah responded to Eli.

Instead of getting defensive, Hannah was bold but humble. She chose to be vulnerable and set the record straight. By choosing the high road, her posture ended up facilitating favor with God and a blessing from the priest, whose perception of her had completely changed. Hannah soon found herself pregnant with a boy she would name Samuel, which means "heard by God."

I think accolades are in order for Eli too. He actually listened to Hannah and recanted once he understood her heart. Not all leaders would have done so. We all read each other wrong at some point, but what we do after we get it wrong will be the difference between our voices spreading *hooray* or provoking hardship because of our misinformed opinions.

HOW WE CAN HELP

I have to be honest here. I felt a little relieved after I read Hannah's story. Did you? After all, if a devout follower of God, working for decades to guide people to the Lord, misreads a situation and throws *booray* instead of *hooray*, then you know we're gonna too.

Assumptions are tricky. I don't know why Eli confused Hannah's prayer with drunkenness. His workplace was where people came to pour their hearts out to God! But who am I to judge? I'm someone who comes by assumptions easily. Even knowing the old adage that says "Assume makes an ass out of u and me" (ass-u-me, get it?) hasn't stopped my keen ability to tell myself a good story without needing all the details.

Maybe you're a little like that too. If you've ever been quick to respond with an answer before you've asked a question, or if you've sat as superior over someone and set a label on top of them, we both could learn from 1 Samuel 1 and sit less like Eli and offer more like Hannah. The last thing we need to be doing as Christ's representatives is to be making judgments that are belittling or false.

No matter what your Enneagram number is, where you land on the Myers-Briggs scale, or how you score on the StrengthsFinder test, practicing such biblical behavior will help each of us navigate our way around a conversation, if not a crowd, a little bit better.

Here's the bottom line. We need to be as clear as we can with others while realizing we all have different filters and sometimes are speaking a whole different language. Cheer won't always translate. We just need to do our best and take a chance. It's a must for God's people.

Here's a question. When someone does try to lend some encouragement or throw confetti and they end up missing, are you the person who gives the benefit of the doubt and believes the best? If that's your tendency, I bet you're killing it when it comes to confetti throwing. Most of us have to have a good wrestle with ourselves before we can believe the best.

We make bad judges. If we end up unlucky and find ourselves in the judgment seat, or if we're called to play the part of the jury and rule on someone else's misfortune, we need to remember Jesus's words from Matthew 7:2: "You'll receive the same judgment you give. Whatever you deal out will be dealt out to you" (CEB).

That's a scary enough thought to convince me. I'll stay perfectly content sitting in my wingback, letting God issue what's next for somebody rather than me. He already knows their end from the beginning anyway. I have enough trouble just dealing with me and mine on a daily basis, so I really don't have time to play referee for others.

Besides, it is way more fun in the cheering section. People are pumped over there. So I say, let go of the gavel and save your voice for the sidelines. I'll gladly clap for the ones God has put in the game, whether I'm running next to them or watching at a distance while I offer my cheer. We've all got work to do, and we need help getting there.

WHEN IT'S A MISS

Once when I was a kid, I rode my bike home from a friend's house. I was a couple of houses away from mine when something made me look behind for a split second—enough time to crash smack into my neighbor's parked car. That's what comes to mind when I think of what a miss can feel like. You're movin' along, going in the right direction, and bam! What the heck just jolted me? Instead of riding in smooth, you end up walking your bike the rest of the way.

(I was fine, by the way. And my kind neighbor, who was out mowing his lawn and saw everything, pretended he didn't so as not to embarrass me. Wasn't that nice of him?)

When we are trying to extend some *hooray* to someone and be a voice that matches God's, we are going to stumble around or we're going to just plain miss. Plenty of us are doing the best we can, trying to love God and love His people, but we end up getting it wrong. As you're probably catching on, I can stand first in line as an example of this.

I don't mind because it illustrates how badly we need Jesus. If we could do everything perfectly, Jesus would not be a part of our lives. I'm comforted by all the people I read about in Scripture who kept falling down as they tried to do the right thing. They would try to uphold love and live low (humbly) as God asks. They kept getting back up, but they still had a lot of bruises.

I'm simply pointing out that we can be full of faith, have great affection for God, and really get it wrong. Go easy on yourself.

STILL A MISS

If you look closely at the crew of guys Jesus handpicked, taught, chastised, mentored, and encouraged, you'll see something consistent. The stories in the Gospels are full of the disciples' swings, misses, and full-on strikeouts. It's amazing since we know these were the people Jesus was going to hand the baton to after He left this earth, giving them the mandate to spread the Good News that God is accessible to us.

Yet, even after three years of listening to His parables, watching Him heal, and learning all about His Kingdom, the boys were a bit dim when it came to confetti. For example, in Luke 9, they were reporting about their trips around the country to share about Jesus. They rolled up on some people who happened to be using the name of Jesus to free people bound by demons. John was missing it.

> "Master," said John, "we saw someone driving out demons in your name and we tried to stop him, because he is not one of us." (Luke 9:49)

Issuing freedom isn't only for the all-star team, John. It's for any person who chooses to partner with God and extend help. Confetti can't fall just from the main stage.

If we leave it up to the "professionals," a lot of people will miss out. God has placed each of us strategically next to people just so we can extend *hooray* to the hearts that need it.

A little while later, Jesus and His crew were planning to visit a specific town, but they learned they were not welcome. Both John and James, the two disciples described as closest to Jesus, reacted this way: "Do you want us to call fire down from heaven to destroy them?" (Luke 9:54).

I'd definitely call this a miss, guys.

How is it that their responses to people they didn't see eye to eye with seemed to always get them a direct word of correction from our King instead of applause? Maybe we should do a little reevaluating of our own. What are our reactions when things don't seem fair or when we're next to people we might deem "not getting it"?

I have a heart that I think wants good things for others. But in all honesty, it seems to need a lot more supervision than I once thought. Could we be like the first followers who walked close to Jesus and yet misinterpreted a lot of what He said (and therefore extended the wrong message)?

This isn't a question of particular doctrine or theology. I'm talking about the things written in red that came out of His mouth. Are we getting it or are we missing it? Think of Peter, who was a close friend to Jesus and for three years walked with Him and listened closely to His words—and still rebuked Him *and* denied Him three times. That was a major miss, if there ever was one. And it makes me wonder what I might be missing.

The good news is that in each of these cases, there is a resolve that's found in the voice of Jesus. Whether it's correction and guidance He's giving or encouragement to try again, the voice of our Lord is directing and echoing in the ears of His servants. If we can be flexible and learn to pivot, then we can learn to transition in the midst of any kind of bad translation.

FROM TRANSLATION TO TRANSITION

Remember *communication* and *commotion*? Here's another play on words. Look at *transition* and *translation*. Just two letters swapped for one. That little change can mark the difference in how we get back on track with any misstep we may have taken.

Let me explain. Do you know basketball? Even if you don't, you'll be able to picture this. Say we're playing basketball and you've passed me the ball. But I've come to a standstill because I've made all the steps I'm allowed to make in this play. My only option will be to pivot. When I pivot, more options are now open to me. That means I can transition even though I am standing still. One foot needs to stay planted while the other is mobile and able to move in a new direction to get a look from a different angle.

The same is true in conversation or when we try to extend *hooray* to someone who God might be showing us. When our words or acts don't connect, we can pivot and try to see from a better angle. We can get into a better position to communicate *hooray* in the right translation.

A miss in translation requires us to transition. I view that re-placement "i" as symbolic. Isn't an "I" often the problem? How *I* interpret something or someone and how my *eye* chooses to see can mean the world of difference between winning and losing with others.

In 2 Kings 6 there was a battle approaching. One of the Prophet Elisha's servants was terrified because he could see from his position on a hill that they were about to lose this fight. They didn't have the numbers. Sweat was building up on his forehead as he cried out, "Oh, my master, what are we to do?" (2 Kings 6:15 csb).

Elisha was a prophet with keen understanding about the spirit realm. Without skipping a beat he answered,

> "Don't be afraid," the prophet answered. "Those who are with us are more than those who are with them."

> And Elisha prayed, "Open his eyes, Lord, so that he may see." Then the Lord opened the servant's eyes, and he looked and saw the hills full of horses and chariots of fire all around Elisha. (2 Kings 6:16-17)

We are less afraid when we can see a bigger picture and have greater understanding about our circumstances because God opens our eyes. By the way, prophets help pave the way for that. They have a distinct ability to hear from the heart of God and elevate the whisper. They close the gap between unseen realms as they translate what heaven is up to. We need God's Word to help us win wars. The words God initiates for our lives give us hope, strength, and courage. Prophetic words can walk us through all kinds of hard things; I'm so grateful God gives them not only to our prophets but to all people.

As the story continues, the enemy that was attacking Elisha was struck by God with a physical blindness simply at Elisha's request. An enemy army that couldn't see let Elisha and his servant win a seemingly unwinnable war. Later, God would open the enemy's eyes back up based on another word from Elisha. Lesson: when we want to see something done, the first thing we have to do is ask God.

How we see things will always affect how we make our next move. In this case, Elijah's *I* was changed and his perspective shifted when his eyes were opened to see something different. We will need to pivot plenty in life; the more flexible we are, the easier it is. It helps to have people beside us who can help us actually see.

PIVOT

Brian and I work with people from all over the world who are pastors, songwriters, authors, nonprofit leaders, and Kingdom influencers. They all differ in various degrees on who they interpret Jesus to be and what walking with God is supposed to look like. There can be beauty in individual expressions of faith, and the variety can be wonderful. Yet, there can be contradictions. Certainly, the many manifestations of how to interpret the Bible text, and therefore the heart of God, have led to disagreements, divisions, injustices, and even wars.

Human beings seem to be good at not translating God clearly or correctly.

The most dramatic illustration of this was when God the Son Himself stood right in front of well-educated leaders called Pharisees, who preached God to their people and studied incessantly about a coming Messiah. Their interpretation of God's rules and prophecies, though, blinded them. They missed God while they were staring into His face. Their context about Him was out of order; their professional duty to uphold the law left them with no room but to transition incorrectly when the fulfillment of the law they taught walked right in front of them.

Of course, others missed Him too. Generations had been talking about the coming Savior, yet when He grew up right in front of them, but not in the way they expected, they rejected all His miracles, healings, deliverances, biblical teaching, and fulfillments of prophecy. The Apostle John reported after Jesus's death and resurrection that "He was in the world, and though the world was made through him, the world did not recognize him. He came to that which was his own, but his own did not receive him" (John 1:10-11).

That's quite a monumental loss in translation, isn't it? The scriptures they had been studying weren't translating into their hearts, so they couldn't transition their thoughts. It's one thing to have information about Jesus; it's another thing to let that knowledge pivot us toward action.

I would hope that, in a similar historical and cultural context, I would have considered pivoting if I had observed a spiritually powerful rabbi Who claimed to be King die and then rise from the dead, and Who showed Himself to more witnesses than Lewis and Clark ever had. How about you?

We all have to make a decision at some point to sort through our own generations of religion, family paradigms of belief, opinions, influence, experience, disappointments, and disapproval when it comes to our choice to be flexible and pivot in our views about Who Jesus is.

One of the last scenes before Jesus died dramatically illustrates pivot. Two men hung on crosses on either side of Jesus, waiting for death. One of them hurled insults at Jesus. The other pivoted.

> "We are punished justly, because we're getting back what we deserve for the things we did, but this man has done nothing wrong." Then he said, "Jesus, remember me when you come into your kingdom."

And Jesus said to him, "Truly I tell you, today you will be with me in paradise." (Luke 23:41-43 CSB)

I think for many people, the ultimate destination of paradise is, at this moment, just a pivot away. It's a decision, a declaration, a confession, a submission, or a repentance. It's not something that always seems that life-changing, but if practiced will actually prove to be life-altering.

SUBMISSION

All right, I snuck the *S* word in. Did you catch that? Maybe the double-take gave you whiplash. I recognize that submission is not a popular topic. But it needs to be talked about.

When the word is broken up, it's really something beautiful. The *sub* prefix means "under." Put it together with *mission*. The combination means under the mission of a superior.

In the Greek, the word for submission is *hupotasso*. It means "to arrange yourself under in an orderly fashion." It's a military term, coming from a place of safety and protection.

Submission in the right context, then, doesn't take our voice away from us. It protects us and creates order.

I like order. It makes me feel safe. That may be why submission hasn't ever been much of a problem for me.

I'm not saying that God is necessarily "safe," in the sense of cautious or predictable. No, He's wild and adventurous! But I know I can trust the One Who hung the stars to also be the One Who directs my next steps. I have no problem bending low for Someone Who gives the ocean a boundary line and controls the waves with His finger (see Isaiah 40:12).

What about you? What happens when the translation failure happens between you and the One Who hung the stars?

DISAPPOINTMENT

Trying to navigate through hurt, pain, or confusion can be like driving in the dark without Google Maps to a place you've never been before. I second-guess myself and my surroundings when I'm in the dark.

Hooray is a challenge when I'm feeling lost or can't see where I am stationed in life.

Remember Joseph? The one who sat in a prison cell after he'd been given the picture of a promise? His promise came through a dream that left out a lot of details. It would be easy to assume that things were "lost in translation" between Joseph and God, but that was not the case. Joseph just didn't have the whole picture.

I can imagine how dark things might have seemed to him. But he was faithful to steward what *was* given him. Once he was able to interpret one of Pharaoh's dreams, he quickly climbed the ladder of success. Then he did not hesitate to throw confetti on Pharoah by operating in the wisdom of God and extending his gift.

Not every prison story ends as well. Think of John the Baptist (see Mark 1:1-8). Eccentric in dress, wild in nature, John was born for one single purpose: to prepare the way for the Lord.

His name means "God is gracious." The concept may have provided assurance to his parents, who had him at an old age. But I wonder if, after unfairly landing inside some cell doors, John may have struggled with it a bit. Even being Jesus's cousin gave John no special divine pass when it came to the tribulation he was facing. He previously had told his followers, when Jesus came on the scene, that "he must become greater; I must become less" (John 3:30). He had no idea that prophecy would come true very soon.

Our submission to Jesus overrides our rights when it comes to what's fair. Maybe that's what stops most of us from wholeheartedly following Jesus. We think that if we stay in the car and hand over the wheel to a driver who's invisible, we are sure to lose control. Some people might find themselves too practical for that kind of scenario, too scared of that scenario, or right in the middle of that scenario.

When I feel scared, things tend to turn inward quickly. All the questions get internalized. *Why me? What did I do? Why is this so hard? How did it turn out like this? Have I not done enough, given enough, gone low enough? When is it going to be enough?*

When I look at John's situation in the cell, I'm sobered by the realization that Jesus doesn't have to answer to any of us, though in His kindness He sometimes does. John the Baptist sent Jesus a direct question: "Are you the one who is to come, or should we expect someone else?" (John 7:19). Jesus chose to answer His cousin with one of heaven's loudest messages.

> The blind receive sight, the lame walk, those who have leprosy are cleansed, the deaf hear, the dead are raised, and the good news is proclaimed to the poor. (John 7:22)

Does that sound like confetti? What Jesus reported didn't move John out of his locked cell or prevent his death. No one knows if it brought John any comfort. I imagine it did, shifting his thinking and reassuring him against whatever doubts and lies were troubling him.

Hooray might not always feel helpful, but when truth is extended, lies can at least be silenced. We have to determine if it is enough to hand over the wheel, stay in the cell, and continue in the faith.

WHAT'S NEXT?

Just three months after being newly married to my darling husband, he was in a car accident with his younger sister. Brian was driving a Geo Metro, and that tiny piece of tin didn't stand a chance against a lady running a red light at full speed. When her car crashed into them, his head went through the windshield. Then he spun around, and his head ended up through the side window.

At the hospital, Brian was awake and verbal, and introduced me to the doctor as his fiancée. I was tempted to make up a great story with my new blank slate, but things got serious as the doctor went over what might be coming next.

In the weeks after he was released, Brian was diagnosed with major depression as a result of his major brain injury. "I could have told you that weeks ago," I said under my breath. He was sleeping all the time. He was irritable and unmotivated. Our sex life was nil. All these things were in direct contradiction to the person I stood at the altar with to say, "I do, I will, and I promise to."

This was quite a "lost in translation" moment for me and God. It took a minute for me to wrestle with our new reality and try to filter my new context about what life would be like. I think in general most of us try to negotiate how much "less" of ourselves we will become; the call to pick up our cross and follow Christ is not something I want to be shouting in a megaphone to others about. It's not all that appealing, and it doesn't seem to beckon people to want to come and follow after our God.

It's not glamorous and it's the very opposite of easy, so when life handed me a car accident and my new circumstance had the word *depression* stamped over the coming season, I had only two options: give in or give up.

I'm a competitive person, thank goodness, so giving up wasn't an option. I gave in to the message Jesus shared, and I bent my knee under the weight of what was ours to carry. I trusted the words He said, that if I really lost my life for Him, then I would be sure to find it (see Matthew 10:39).

Three years later we got to tell a story about a miraculous healing and divine intervention because of obedience, prayer, and fasting. I'm not ignorant to the fact that not all stories end like that. Not every heart hears or receives what it wants to. It's a painful dilemma when we can't report a good outcome after begging for something we so badly need.

Maybe that's why Jesus left John with such sobering words: "God blesses those who do not fall away because of me" (Mathew 11:6 NLT). Gulp, I don't know how I'd swallow that sitting there in prison after using my life to pave the way for Jesus. Those words, after John gave his life to point others toward the God Who came for us. How can we be *hooray* to others when we are hurting?

Here's what I know. God's promise is to be with us and to be present beside us no matter where we go or what we're walking through. He can turn any ending into a new beginning and use any kind of bad, hard, or broken story and turn it upward. He is good all of the time, no matter our circumstance or situation. He doesn't hand out disease and disappointment, and though I wish He healed the first time every person asked, and I wish He worked the way we wanted Him to on the timeline in which we needed Him to, God doesn't conform to us. He hears us, He's moved by us, certainly He's gone to great lengths to reveal His love to us, but the message He had to carry on His back for us caused Him to sweat drops of blood, and His promise was that we too would face hardship if we choose to walk in His ways.

So if you're feeling a little in the dark with your interpretation of Him or you're having a hard time trying to translate what He's up to, remember that when you lose your life, you will feel actual loss at times. When you bend low to the ground to make yourself less so that He can become more, you will feel sore in places you didn't know it could hurt. But in all that losing and lowering of yourself, there will be a lot of lifting up and finding yourself because that's a promise too. He is faithful and good and just, and His mercy is here to meet us each new day with enough grace measured for whatever is about to come into our lives. So chin up, not all prison doors stay closed.

Joseph had to walk through a nightmare, but he got to see his promise take shape in due time.

WE DON'T KNOW
THE WHOLE STORY

There is one last story I have to tell about prison doors. It's about two guys who followed the path of Christ and ended up sitting in a cell with no idea what was going to happen next.

Paul and Silas had justification to feel scorn and sadness toward God, and who would blame them? Instead, they turned another direction in their hearts and ended up being right in the middle of a miracle.

> About midnight Paul and Silas were praying and singing hymns to God, and the other prisoners were listening to them. Suddenly there was such a violent earthquake that the foundations of the prison were shaken. At once all the prison doors flew open, and everyone's chains came loose. (Acts 16:25-26)

Prisons look different to each of us. Some people's prisons are decorated with sleek granite, muted walls, and fashionable wallpaper. We don't always know how locked up people are right beside us. Thankfully "midnight" still marks the start of new days, new decades, and new lives. Our "suddenly" could be just a song away.

When Paul and Silas chose to praise instead of pout, it opened up doors and it changed everything. Their choice to harmonize with *hooray* didn't only free themselves but also those who sat next to them.

Meditation

If you are in a "lost in translation" moment with God or another person, don't be afraid to ask for clarity. The answer is not guaranteed, of course, but you can take comfort knowing that you are doing your part as you wait for the other party to respond.

So with that in mind, let's ponder this thought:
- How do you usually respond in the midst of obscurity with God or others?

REFLECTION

"I know that you can do all things; no purpose of yours can be thwarted." (Job 42:2)

6

Fan Club

*They may forget what you said,
but they will never forget how
you made them feel.*

—Carl W. Buehner[1]

CHEER

I love to find myself in a good cheering section. It's exhilarating to join in roars of approval, my heart pounding, all my energy directed toward one thing.

I was a soccer player in college. But at the University of North Dakota in Grand Forks back then, there wasn't much to report when it came to the women's NCAA Division II fan base—aside from the great players and the coaches who trained them. The cheering section was always pretty thin.

But men's Division I hockey? That's another story. I'll be honest and tell you that I am not a huge hockey fan. But it sure was easy to get swept up in all the excitement at hockey games. I never painted my face green and white or bought a Fighting Hawks jersey, much to the disapproval of some of my classmates. But participating in the explosive crowd of cheering fans was fun.

My husband once returned from a Texas A&M football game where he said he discovered not just fans but fanatics. A fanatic has excessive zeal, obsessive interest, and limitless enthusiasm for something. (I'd bet that, at that, any self-respecting Aggie would yell, "Well, duh!") Brian said it was absolutely exhilarating to be in the bleachers amidst that maroon mob that really knew how to cheer. Fair-weather fans are a dime a dozen. The loyal Aggie school spirit stays in it for the long haul with painted faces while the snow is falling. That is really something.

All this makes me wonder what our churches would look like if they were filled with fans who had the same kind of enthusiasm for one another. What would happen if the applause we had for our brothers and sisters was as loud, fun, and encouraging as the way we shout out for athletes?

Could we band our voices together for goals way more important and longer-lasting than anything happening on a playing field and showing up on a scoreboard?

FANS

Refuge Foundation creates a space where for four or five days we become the best and most loyal fans of anybody that God brings to our property. But we couldn't exist without our ministry staff. To say these mostly twentysomethings make the celebration happen would be a ridiculous understatement. I wouldn't trade it because these millennial darlings are beyond exceptional. However, they are also very messy.

I don't just mean the mess of not putting their stuff away, or not taking regular showers, although that does occur. I'm talking about the mess of sorting through self and selfishness as they put others' needs ahead of their own, again and again. These gems are nothing short of gold, but there is a lot of refinement that has to happen before they can sparkle.

Day in and day out, they serve, care for, and clean up after our guests. I am in awe of their service as they hug, laugh, pray, and root for whomever God puts in front of them. A lot of time they get very little sleep; often they get very little thanks. Along with all that daily dying to self can come a heap of frustration.

It's hard work being a fan. Carrying a load of confetti for others can be exhausting.

My Refuge crew reminds me of a passage in Mark, where Jesus and His disciples had just crossed the Sea of Galilee.

As soon as they got out of the boat, people recognized Jesus. They ran throughout that whole region and carried the sick on mats to wherever they heard he was. And wherever he went—into villages, towns or countryside—they placed the sick in the marketplaces. They begged him to let them touch even the edge of his cloak, and all who touched it were healed. (Mark 6:54-56)

There will come a season in which each of us will have the opportunity to run so that others can be in the presence of Jesus and receive a touch from Him. Don't be deceived, though. Running is hard, even if you're good at it. The process involves cross-carrying and knee-bending because you can't lay people on mats without humbling yourself. But every time you do, it's a chance to see the miraculous happen.

Once we have encountered our own touch from God and we've had some healing ourselves, then we can choose to pick up *hooray* like those in Mark 6—good fans who grab mats and help get others in front of Jesus.

Jesus spoke some incredible, and incredibly difficult, words to us when He said, "If any of you wants to be my follower, you must give up your own way, take up your cross daily, and follow me" (Luke 9:23 NLT). When we follow Him, we are asked to put down our own agendas and pick up His. We are to let Him direct our steps as we walk in His ways.

Followers of Jesus are implored to be fans of others because we are a reflection of Him. We are to reflect a God Who is good, fun, kind, generous, caring, gracious, and loving. We are to reflect and conform to His image, even when conforming is not comfortable.

THE FATHER OF FANS

Jesus told a story about a party a father decided to throw for his son. It was a pretty crazy situation. Here's what happened.

The man's youngest son had demanded his inheritance and took off with it when the father obliged. We don't know how much time went by, but it was long enough for the boy to squander all his money in wild living and make a terrible mess of his life. He was out of options and starving. He finally made a good decision.

> I will set out and go back to my father and say to him: Father, I have sinned against heaven and against you. I am no longer worthy to be called your son; make me like one of your hired servants. (Luke 15:18-19)

He must have been so nervous. I'll bet he practiced that apology a million times as he limped his way back. I know I've rehearsed apologies for far less crimes. But from the way Jesus told it, it seems obvious that this boy didn't know his father very well.

> But while his son was still a long way off, his father saw him and was filled with compassion for him; he ran to his son, threw his arms around him and kissed him. (Luke 15:20)

Men in that culture were too dignified to run, but this father ran. Then, instead of punishing or rejecting the son, the father embraced him. He barely listened to the practiced apology—he was too busy covering his son's face with kisses. The father didn't stop there. He called his servants to bring the son the best robe, a ring, and a brand-new pair of shoes. He ordered his cook to prep some T-bones and all the trimmings for a feast. Confetti was flying like fireworks as they hired a band and began to celebrate—because he "was dead and is alive again; he was lost and is found" (Luke 15:24).

This is a father who understood extravagant love and the value of celebration. This beloved son was not only going to finally eat a full meal, he was going to be reinstated with an incredible party.

This father is a picture of God the Father, whom Jesus came to reveal. He is the God Who has *hooray* in His voice and confetti in His hands. God is our fan.

The story has so much to teach us, primarily about the heart of God toward His kids, the grace He extends, and His beautiful pursuit of us. And when we match our voices to His and align our hearts with heaven, we too will be people who throw parties for those who get it wrong instead of acting like party poopers.

OLDER SIBLING SYNDROME

The scene in Luke 15 between the father and the "prodigal son" made no initial mention of the older brother. When Jesus finally brought him into the story, it was clear that Son No. 1 was no fan of his reprobate brother and could see no reason to throw confetti at his return. Not only that, he resented anyone else doing it.

Here we have a picture of fan fallout, something that can happen to us all, and from which we need to know how to recover.

The party must have been going exceptionally well because the brother could hear it as he came in from the fields. Once back at the house, he grabbed a servant and demanded to know what was going on.

> "Your brother has come," he replied, "and your father has killed the fattened calf because he has him back safe and sound." (Luke 15:27)

I have to admit that every time I read this story, I have empathy for the older brother, not only because I am an eldest child but also because I am prone to keeping score. It's easy to let "principle" and "fairness" be our only lens. That may not be all that was going on with the angry older brother. But certainly some. Listen to him tell his dad off.

> The older brother became angry and refused to go in. So his father went out and pleaded with him. But he answered his

father, "Look! All these years I've been slaving for you and never disobeyed your orders. Yet you never gave me even a young goat so I could celebrate with my friends. But when this son of yours who has squandered your property with prostitutes comes home, you kill the fattened calf for him!" (Luke 15:28-30)

I can just picture him, nose to nose with Dad, waving his arms or shoving his finger in his father's chest. I'll bet he was ranting about how unfair the celebration was and why his irresponsible younger brother didn't "deserve" any kind of a party at all. Older brother syndrome in full bloom.

No doubt the lens of fairness has robbed me of seeing the good that God is up to in the lives of others. It has stopped me from seeing His hand redeem lives and restore relationships. I guess at the end of the day we need to ask ourselves if we want to be the kind of people who demand fairness or shoot off fireworks.

Thank goodness I have a new lens that can see through the grace that has been bestowed to me. When I forget about what God has done and what He's forgiven, I start looking like the older brother and demanding fairness.

I think that's the hardest part about *hooray*. It calls us to see people through love and grace. It challenges us to put on a more generous lens than what we're used to looking through. It reveals the thoughts and opinions of our hearts, and it changes the meaning of fair.

For a recovering finger-pointer, I'm telling you this is hard living sometimes. When we are fans first, we have to leave fair up to God, and that enables us to serve and party without any worry.

Could we lose the older brother act? Could we be the kind of people who come with confetti when we see God making plans for a party? I hate to think what might have happened had the older brother looked up and spotted his brother before his father did.

MOVE ALONG

Jesus didn't tell us whether or not the older brother ever had a change of heart. While that bothers me, I know it's realistic.

Not everyone responds to a father's love, nor the Father's love. There are a lot of people who choose to stay out in the fields and pout, and not show up for anybody. There are a lot of people who can't compliment or won't congratulate. A simple "thank you" from their lips would be like moving a mountain. You get them a nice coffee mug and drop a gift card inside—and silence. Okay, I'm digressing now.

The truth is, people disappoint us, they hurt us, and they walk away from us. Sometimes it's because of their own stuff, and sometimes it's because we have disappointed, hurt, and walked away from them. At least that's true in the story we read.

So, not everyone in God's family is willing to pick up pom-poms and participate with applause over your life, but that doesn't change how we can party. We've just gotta keep moving along.

Plenty of people showed up to eat some steak and cut a rug in celebration of the prodigal son coming home. Let's do our best to lock eyes with the ones who show up and stop losing sleep over the ones who don't join the party. Some people just don't know how to move with the music that's playing over your life.

Our best days and defining moments will not be measured by how many people decide to clap for us. On our good, bad, and worst days, we have a God Who is present and active on our behalf. He's wooing, speaking, and unveiling in these present moments, and no matter what we've done, where we've been, or where we're headed, He comes for us. He comes with streamers. He comes to meet with us, hold us, scold us, and speak to us like a good father would: like the Good Father He is. That's worth toasting.

FANS, FOLLOWERS, & FAVORITES

In social media, we're surrounded by fans, followers, and favorites. It's a challenging dynamic. We don't need to know someone very well to be a fan or a follower. We have followers who only "know" us in cyberspace, fans who are not necessarily our followers, and favorites we aren't fans of or even follow. It's not just a mouthful, it's also a lot to navigate.

When we add in following Jesus, it can get really complicated. Being a fan, follower, and favorite of Jesus has a way of drawing a line in the sand. The sacred beliefs we hold sometimes bruise the ones we love or are trying to applaud. Sometimes we get bruised by their views too.

When that happens, we need to remember that acceptance is different from agreement. We don't need to agree with others to be able to sit close, virtually or in person. We can continue to love others, no matter where they stand on things. Our supporting and honoring them do not negate our own stand on what God has said and what He's asked us to do.

Same thing among fellow followers of God—maybe even more importantly. I've sat across from brothers and sisters, just talking or posting, wondering, agreeing or disagreeing over views on marriage and homosexuality, demons and deliverance, how God's gifts could be used today, and a myriad of other controversial issues. These discussions have provoked a slew of emotions: laughter, frustration, anger. There have been plenty of intense moments as hearts are pricked and feelings hurt. Yet we remain mutual fans. That allows us to work toward getting ahold of ideas we are still trying to work out in our faith and expressing them the best we can—and listening as the other person does the same.

We don't all agree on topics in the Bible. But I think we can agree to see one another through the same lens of love that God looks through. Not just *can*, we *must*. We must stand in love and hold space for grace. I think we'd be more careful about what our lips say and what our fingers type if we remember that there is a divine image bearer on the other side of the screen or the other side of the table whose heart is worth protecting.

Remember, Jesus managed to tick off a ton of people with His views while remaining kind and loving as He healed, preached, and brought people toward God.

Next time you're online or in line at your favorite coffeehouse, remind yourself it is your great privilege to serve and build up the people you are in spaces with. We can become fans of just about anyone, turning favorites into friends and helping folks become followers of Christ.

WHAT A FAN

Fans help us see our way through things. My dear friend Jess had suffered a miscarriage. In the week her baby had been expected, Jess showed up to celebrate our other pregnant friend at her baby shower. No one would have blamed Jess for not coming. That kind of party under those kinds of circumstances surely could bring up pain and feelings that no fan of Jess's would wish her to go through.

She showed up anyway, not to sulk or envy or seek sympathy (only a few of us knew about the heartache she carried that day) but to call forth her cheer for someone else. She tossed fairness out the window and chose to be a fan for another. She threw confetti just by her presence and applauded even though it hurt. She saw a good God Who was doing a good thing in the life of a friend—and she showed up with balloons.

I'm not sure I could have managed. I'm not sure I could have put on a new lens that day, one that wouldn't be clouded by my grief and sense of loss, a lens that could see the joy in God bringing forth something good for another.

We should all be so lucky to have someone in our corner who would hold that kind of a space for *hooray* over us. Could we be ones who would go to such lengths to carry encouragement for others and call our cheer to rise in the midst of our own pain and uncertainty?

That's a fan, going to lengths to put another before self while getting ahold of God's heart. We have a mandate as fans, friends, and followers of Jesus, a final list of instructions given by Jesus and left to us that we would go and make disciples. We are to express the heart of the Father by showing, telling, and displaying powerful works that bring forward His Kingdom (see Matthew 28:16-20). How we choose to express and extend the mandate we are called to bring will have unique variety. Sometimes that will simply mean we show up for each other, and sometimes it will require more.

WAR STORIES

Following Jesus comes with hardships and heartaches as well as *hoorays*. That's not something I'm just saying. Listen to Jesus Himself.

> I have told you these things, so that in me you may have peace. In this world you will have trouble. But take heart! I have overcome the world. (John 16:33)

We all face troubles, whether on the home front from those we love, on a battlefield out in the world, or somewhere in between. My prayer is that when we face those battles, we have friends and fans to stand beside us and lock arms with.

There is a story of a war that gets won because a follower of God had the support of others. Yes, Moses had faith and was obedient to God. But God used two friends to come alongside Moses when he most needed it.

In Exodus 17, the Israelites were facing a fight they hadn't asked for or prepared for. Moses proposed an odd strategy. He told his buddy Joshua to grab all the strong guys he could and get down to the battlefield. Meanwhile, Moses would climb a nearby hill and hold up his staff toward heaven. He must have been inspired because as long as Moses held his hands high, the people of God prevailed. When his arms got tired and he lowered them, the enemy took over.

What happened next is beautiful. Two men came beside him.

> Moses' hands were heavy. So they took a stone and put it under
> him, and he sat on it; and Aaron and Hur supported his hands,
> one on one side and one on the other. So his hands were steady
> until the sun set. And Joshua defeated Amalek and his people
> with the edge of the sword. (Exodus 17:12-13 NASB)

I wish the passage had a few more details. Was it Moses who called
Aaron and Hur over to help him, or did they just come? Did the
men first see the need and then have to convince Moses that it
wasn't weakness to accept help?

We are only privy to the outcome and the lesson we can glean
from it: we aren't to face life's battles alone, not literally and not
spiritually either. We need strong hands beside us that are willing
to help us, to help us stretch our arms toward heaven and call on
the things we hope to have.

Oftentimes, though, we try to muscle through things with just an
army of one. When we don't share our pain, disappointment, or
the war stories that leave us bruised, we feel alone.

We were created in the image of a triune God Who did not create
the world alone, nor does He stand alone now. Relationship is
His good idea, and any close one will take courage, honesty, and
vulnerability. It will also be what helps us get to victory.

Offering our presence is a great ministry. I feel grateful to have
supportive friends who follow after God and aren't deterred by
anyone's neediness. These are gals who are able to see the struggle
in each other and help hold up an arm when it's necessary. That
can be to say a prayer, paint a room, clean a house, watch a kid,

bring a meal, offer some insight, clap her hands—whatever the holding might mean in the moment.

Everyone's arms get heavy. In fact, we get downright exhausted at times. Do not be afraid to unburden your heart to trusted friends. It is a sacred work to listen, grieve, cheer, and receive from the ones God has put next to us. In fact, asking for some assistance only seems to grow the hearts of comrades closer.

Think of Saul's son Jonathan, who decided to rout an enemy outpost by himself, accompanied by his armor-bearer (and God, of course). He was an experienced warrior, but I still wonder if he was looking for some assurance when he described the plan to his armor-bearer. He got it.

> Jonathan: "*Perhaps the LORD will act in our behalf. Nothing can hinder the LORD from saving, whether by many or by few.*" Armor-bearer: "*Do all that you have in mind. I am with you heart and soul.*" (1 Samuel 14:6-7)

Presence evokes confidence. Sometimes all we need is for someone to stand next to us while we share our vision, wrestle through heartache, or open up about the worries we have as we try to run with our next idea. Jonathan ended up winning that battle even though it was two against a whole team.

I'd be remiss if I didn't circle back to Moses. The arm-holding was a prophetic act (an action we take in the physical realm to partner with what God is doing in the spiritual realm) that led the Israelites to win. I don't know how or why that worked, but, biblically, God often seems to ask others to do things that seem odd or irrational to us, and yet it's what works.

There are so many examples in Scripture. I'll go to another battle that was won through prophetic revelation that on the outside looked absurd. I'm thinking, of course, of Jericho.

In Joshua 6, God gave instructions for the men to march around the city's impenetrable wall for seven days. Then they were to blast a trumpet and give a loud and long battle cry. You probably know what happened. The walls that were keeping them out came tumbling down. No fighting, just marching. I'll bet as the men made their way around the seventh time, they were praying it would work.

Oftentimes God will ask us to declare a victory before we see it, stand to praise when we don't feel like it, and bow in surrender when we have every right to yell. Maybe because it's good for our hearts to do it, maybe it's much more than that.

We get our war strategies from God just like we do everything else, so don't be afraid to do the thing He says. March around, declare a truth to the wind, or get out the oil to raise the dead turkey from the ground (that's a story for another time). He already has our solution. He's just looking for our partnership to bring it about. The next time you decide you are going to go pick a fight, just make sure you don't go alone.

HEROINES OF *HOORAY*

Most of us know stories of incredible heroines. I'm thinking of women like Harriet Tubman, who served as a conductor on the Underground Railroad freeing the enslaved, spied for the Union Army during the Civil War, and worked endlessly for women's voting rights.

We've heard of Mother Teresa, the great nun, missionary, saint, and Nobel laureate who founded the Missionaries of Charity. Launched in India, the organization is now worldwide. They care for people dying of HIV/AIDS, leprosy, and tuberculosis; run soup kitchens; work in orphanages; and offer counseling programs. The nuns make vows to give up their own rights, comfort, and desires to serve the poorest of the poor.

Aimee Semple McPherson was among these incredible women, laboring endlessly in the service of helping people. She was a traveling preacher who founded the Foursquare Church. The first congregation, Angelus Temple in Los Angeles, became the largest for its era. "Sister Aimee," as she was known, gathered people of every faith and fed hundreds of thousands during the Great Depression. Her service unified foreign tongues and anchored people in the faith of a healing God.

These are only snippets about some of my favorites, who held onto *hooray* and threw plenty of confetti around them. Their stories can sometimes leave us feeling like "What could I ever do?" It's hard enough to find a free morning to serve at a soup kitchen, much less start one.

Thankfully, Jesus did not command us to "do as much good as your neighbor does, or more." That's a relief because most of us would quickly be disqualified. I would be, for certain! After all, "not yelling at my kids for the day" is usually on the top of my to-do list. I cannot even consider what other monumental things I'd need to do to earn a gold star.

Nevertheless, I love reading the stories of great heroes and heroines who have responded to God's guidance because it stirs up all kinds of probability in me about what's possible. As long as I don't focus on the gap between what I see other people doing and what I feel I am capable of doing! Our mission as Jesus taught is not to keep a watchful eye on others but to keep settled into Him.

He put no limits on our creativity and what it could look like for us to extend love, care, and help to those in need. Likewise He didn't put any limits on the help He'd give us as we try to move in these different rhythms of care.

UNKNOWN

Tens of thousands of people could potentially be counted as our favorites, but we don't know their names or, in some cases, have never met them. I'm thinking of those we might share seats with at church or pass in our neighborhoods, those doing good work we'll never hear about. Their names will never be listed in books. No one will make movies about them. Even their families might remain ignorant of their generosity and sacrifices.

It reminds me of the Tomb of the Unknown Soldier at Arlington National Cemetery. It represents all unidentified war victims and honors the extending and giving of their lives. The anonymous role they played in history has been felt. Their ultimate sacrifice has ensured our freedom even as their faces will forever remain nameless to us.

Some of us will play parts and have assignments that don't put us center stage. In fact we may not have an audience at all. Some roles are too private or too sacred to be put in front of other people. Others of us will carry messages that need to reach the ears of thousands and stir up their hearts.

Whatever our role is, our motive mustn't be mixed. We don't work and extend for the applause of others; we work to extend an applause in hopes that others will be encouraged.

Kingdom success is not measured by who is watching us, but by the One Who is watching over us. Jesus Himself illustrates this.

When a disciple of Jesus told his friend to come with him so he could see Jesus, his response was, "Can anything good come out of Nazareth?" (John 1:46 CSB). Jesus, God Incarnate Himself, was not recognized by the majority of people He interacted with.

There is another great account in Scripture of the miraculous happening by the "unknown." A man gets healed by Jesus, but he has no clue it was Him. Jesus goes incognito and changes a moment for this man that ultimately ends up changing his whole life.

I think a lot of life change happens in ordinary moments, and this was just another day where Jesus was just another nameless face in the crowd.

We must have eyes wide open in these days. God is writing His messages with the people we sit beside and extending Kingdom invitations through everyday people. Thank goodness for that, because we might not recognize the divine if it were drinking coffee right next to us.

WHO IS HE?

In John 5, we read the story of the paralyzed man who had been lying next to a healing pool called Bethesda for thirty-eight years. *Thirty-eight years!* Wow. When Jesus saw him, He asked him a question: "Do you want to get well?" (John 5:6). His healing would require massive changes in all areas, not just whether he could walk again. He'd have to change his daily habits, patterns, and beliefs. Did he truly want that? Apparently the man finally answered yes, and Jesus obliged by healing him.

Those who knew this man to be in pain for decades could now see him walking around. Naturally the suspicious ones began to ask him about it.

> "Who is this man who told you, 'Pick up your mat and walk'?" they asked. But the man who was healed did not know who it was, because Jesus had slipped away into the crowd that was there. (John 5:12-13 CSB)

In a world where we are used to being seen, where we post pictures about the parties we attend or what we just ate for dinner, I think it's good to be reminded that being known by God but not needing to be known by everyone is smart living. Yes, we need people who know us well, but when our internal highs and lows are being dictated by a media screen because of how many "likes" or comments we've had, then, friends, we need to do some examining. I propose that watching our followers and following after others can make it difficult to follow after the only One Who knows us completely.

If you're finding it difficult to keep your eyes on Jesus because you're indulging in a lot of fanfare, can I propose you take some time to unplug from the follows, the fans, the posts, and the pictures? Your comments and your cheer can continue another day, but for now, let's keep our eyes on the One Who has something to say to us. I'm proposing that for the next week, you try to make a practice of sitting in His presence before posting a picture on social media. Before you follow and comment as a fan, would you choose first to be a friend and be with Him?

Meditation

Consider who in your life might need you to show up in person for them today as a fan. Balloons, cookies, a call, whatever form the confetti needs to look like—would you make some space to let your applause be heard in another heart today?

God is using us, everyday people, to hold up arms, make an impact, and rouse the spirits of those beside us. That's what fans do.

So with that in mind, let's ponder on this thought:
- Who needs your *hooray*?

REFLECTION

"Keep your eyes on Jesus, who both began and finished the race we're in. Study how he did it . . . he never lost sight of where he was headed—that exhilarating finish in and with God." (Hebrews 12:2 MSG)

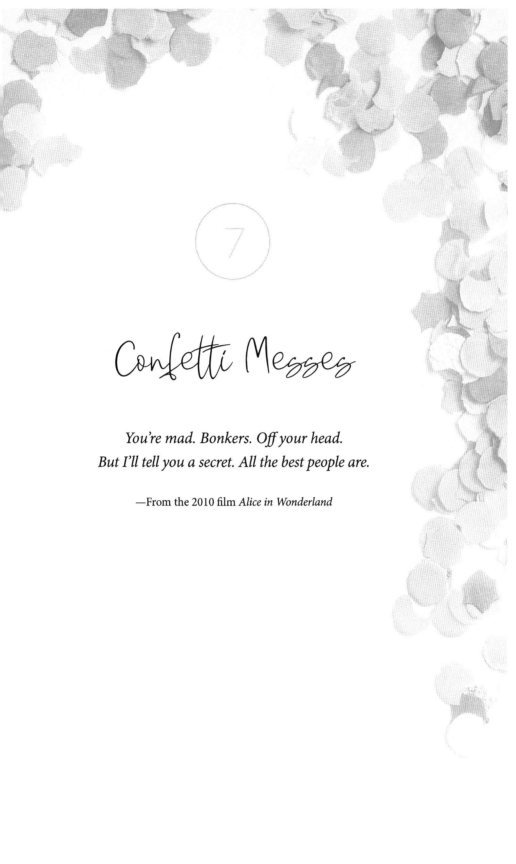

7

Confetti Messes

You're mad. Bonkers. Off your head.
But I'll tell you a secret. All the best people are.

—From the 2010 film *Alice in Wonderland*

BROKEN & FRAGRANT

Confetti is both marvelous and messy.

I recently attended a conference inside a huge arena. At the end of the event, a giant ball dropped from the ceiling, opened up, and spewed sparkle all over us.

It was astonishing and delightful and certainly celebratory. But confetti was everywhere—including places I didn't want it to go!

Do you know what I was thinking? Keep in mind that I'm essentially in the business of cleaning up. Whether it's laundry or words that need sorting through, sheets or mindsets that need to be changed, there is always a daily maintenance that needs to be done. That's probably why all I could think about was what a mess it was going to be for the people who had to pick all of it up.

There are good messes and bad messes and then there are confetti messes. Inevitably, when confetti lands, it leaves a bright, shiny, sparkly pile of untidiness. If we are going to take time to celebrate others by throwing confetti, we had better be prepared for the aftermath. Got your broom ready?

I love the story of the woman who brought her confetti to Jesus in the form of expensive perfume. There are accounts in all four Gospels, although they don't line up identically. Scholars debate whether they're one or three events. Let's just look at Mark 14.

Jesus was reclining at the table and talking with a bunch of His followers when a woman courageously approached. I imagine the whole room went silent as all the surprised men's eyes turned in her direction. But I'll bet she didn't even notice, because she was focused completely on Jesus.

She had purchased the alabaster jar for this act of praise and worship, and with it she bravely let her *hooray* flow.

> She broke the jar and poured it on his head. But some were expressing indignation to one another: "Why has this perfume been wasted?". . . . And they began to scold her. (Mark 14:3-5 CSB)

What a beautiful picture: confetti streaming down the face of Jesus. However, not everyone approved. Maybe no one, except Jesus. (Interesting that as soon as Jesus's disciples started to scold her, Jesus got after them.) This story is a great reminder that our offerings will always cost us. Not everyone will understand what we're doing. There will be believers, onlookers, and mockers who will criticize us as we extend. But we can't hold back because of what people might think.

The mockery of the crowd didn't diminish her act. We still tell her story and look to her example, all these centuries later.

When our gifts get broken, they become all the more fragrant. We humbly offer who we are and what we have been given to the people God has us next to, and as we let Him break us and use us, our aroma becomes more pervasive.

Extending *hooray* is a privilege. When we champion the sons and daughters of God, cheer for their voice, and applaud their call, we are being an extension of God Himself.

However, with all the different kinds of unique people, carrying around different forms of confetti and stewarding applause in different ways, you know there are going to be some messes. There is the mess in our own hearts, the mess of others, and the messes when we are imperfectly trying to offer something life-changing.

The broken jar probably left shards all over the floor, pieces that might pierce others and cause them to stumble. When you get into the business of being with people, of loving them, helping them, and serving them, it gets messy. We can't prevent a confetti mess, but we can stick around for the cleanup. We can follow promptings from the Spirit as best we can and take the next step to extend what God is saying and then let the confetti fall. But have your broom handy.

A MESS OF CONFETTI

Recently I received a group text from a friend. I hadn't had a second cup of coffee yet, so the question hit me like a slap in the face.

Are there any pollutions you see in my life?

Bravo to my friend for her courage in putting such a vulnerable question out there. But to be honest, I was ticked that she would know I had read the text—no hiding since smartphones alert the sender when the message is read—because I was not ready to give her the truthful answer she deserved. I was too scared to.

I could feel the rumbling of confetti about to fall wrong.

My friend was leaning into Proverbs 27:6, believing "wounds from a friend can be trusted." She wanted my help. But I could feel my cool slink toward cowardice.

In my cryptic response, I hid behind generalizations, using phrases like "we all do at times . . ." I was unwilling to "wound" my friend with the truth I saw, even if it would provide her insight and reveal blind spots. I liked where our friendship was, and I didn't know if her heart could take my honest words. So I ducked as if a fastball were coming at my head when I should have stepped forward to swing.

The truth is, she and I are plenty close and have a mutual respect for and trust in one another. That makes my ducking even a bigger mistake. I wasn't brave, and I missed it. In my missing the opportunity to share, my friend missed the opportunity for God to show her some things that could have refined her.

True, in the past my fast tongue has risked plenty of times without being asked, and I'm just thankful I still have friends who sit in my corner and make sure I have a seat next to them. But I backed up from an invitation that would have helped another go forward. No confetti was thrown, no sparkle landed, and therefore no extension of *hooray* was made.

I hate missing. Since this experience, I've determined not to be afraid of a little bit of mess. I just keep my broom a little closer.

On a side note, if you ever find yourself feeling brave and you need some insight on a blind spot, asking a "tell me what you really see" type of question is good practice—if you have wise, loving, and committed friends who see all of you and can share with you in a loving way. I'm not saying make it a regular routine, but at times another angle might be called for when we are trying to get a good look in the mirror.

I can tell you, though, if you decide to reveal a delicate shortcoming in a lovely friend whose heart is not ready and you didn't have permission, there will be a whole lot of mess.

It can be a difficult thing to be the one who has to glide hard words across the table, no matter how good the coffee might be.

We must be careful when hearts are open and vulnerable and we've just been handed a magnifying glass. Having a voice of *hooray* is supposed to help others, which means hard things will need to be said sometimes, but the hard should ultimately lead to helpful for them.

Upon my reflection with my friend, I realized that small invitation has changed me. I'd rather deal with a mess than a miss when it comes to how I want to show up for people. So I've been taking the Apostle Paul's words from Philippians much more seriously.

> [Be] like-minded, having the same love, being one in spirit and of one mind. Do nothing out of selfish ambition or vain conceit. Rather, in humility value others above yourselves, not looking to your own interests but each of you to the interest of the others. (Philippians 2:2-4)

Selfish ambition has to take a back seat to honor and humility every single day. There can be no compromise. It would be best if selfish ambition didn't sit with us at all, but I know this verse is a tall order for any fallen heart. There are all kinds of ways for Paul's words to be put into action when humility is made a practice in our lives and our lens is looking toward the interests of others and not just what our mirrors are reflecting back to us.

Hopefully one day selfish ambition, along with self-protection, will flee for good, and humility will become second nature for us. Honestly, I'd be fine with it being third or fourth nature, as long as it's showing up somewhere recognizable in my life.

When we develop a voice that exudes *hooray*, we will have to intentionally extend ourselves in the direction of another person's good instead of doing what's easy or comfortable for us. Doing nothing out of selfish ambition means that we are to do nothing that is motivated by us gaining an advantage over the benefit or blessing of others . . . as a lifestyle.

Certainly, we have our work cut out for us.

> The heart is deceitful above all things and beyond cure. Who can understand it? I the LORD search the heart and examine the mind, to reward each person according to their conduct, according to what their deeds deserve. (Jeremiah 17:9-10)

We'd be wise to let God do some housekeeping in our hearts on a daily basis. It's clear we can't always judge our own hearts accordingly.

GETTING REAL GETS MESSY

There are, of course, tons of places in Scripture where we can read about Jesus discerning the true needs of a person, no matter what their exterior looks like. I'm thinking of one dramatic scene you've probably heard about, found in John 4.

Jesus and His disciples had been traveling a long time and came to what was known as Jacob's well. They were tired and hungry. The boys went off, leaving Jesus by Himself. I picture Him sitting on a rock wall around the well, head down, taking deep breaths, mopping the sweat from His brow. A solitary woman arrived, carrying her empty water jug, and He asked her for a drink.

Talk about a divine setup. Jesus knew all about this woman. She had spent years sleeping with a string of men, likely conniving them into marriage before getting tossed aside, one after another. Her heart must have been hard as stone and fragile at the same time. Jesus wasted no time getting to the point.

> Everyone who drinks this water will be thirsty again, but whoever drinks the water I give them will never thirst. Indeed, the water I give them will become in them a spring of water welling up to eternal life. (John 4:13-14)

What a "drop the mic" kind of statement from Jesus. The boys should have been there, taking notes and cheering in the background. We can always count on Jesus to tell us the truth, with graciousness and love and without condemnation. The truth is that He came to satiate every part of us, no matter what state our lives are in.

When we have a run-in with the Living God, we will stop running to other things for happiness, wholeness, and completion. After the woman's encounter with Jesus, she left her water jar and ran into the town to tell everyone—including all the folks who had shunned or mocked or hated on her. No doubt she was never the same. That's what our encounters with Jesus will do. They'll provoke change in us and point others toward Him.

An incredible thing about being made in God's image is that He extends to us the same ability to speak something over people that has power for change just by using our words. Remember, at the beginning of time, He spoke nothing into something. When we begin to partner with Him and use timely anointed words, it can change a spirit, heal a heart, and transform the atmosphere around us.

That's how we grow in *hooray*. It has nothing to do with the volume we use or the number of words we have; instead, it's using the right ones at the right time and speaking them forward as God puts them within us.

Call it the prophetic, say it's hearing from God, tell others it came from an idea or a spiritual thought. It doesn't really matter what we name it, so long as we start doing it. Children know how their parents feel about important matters, and as sons and daughters we should get intimately acquainted with how our Father feels about His people. We have the counsel and help of the Holy Spirit, whose role is to give us insight and revelation about what God is thinking.

That partnership provides us with specific words from the heart of God that we get to share with others. So get your hands ready to offer confetti. No matter what kind of situation we find ourselves in, God has something to say about it.

THROWING SEEDS, NOT STONES

Soon after Jesus had the encounter with the woman at the well, He was teaching crowds at the temple in Jerusalem when He met another fallen woman. This time, however, it wasn't a chance meeting, and the conversation was anything but private.

The religious ruling elite, the powerful scribes and Pharisees, had dragged a promiscuous woman into the open square. These were the guys who held up holy laws so ridiculously high that no one could reach them, which meant no one but them could get close to God. They made sure everyone knew it too. They demeaned everyone outside their inner circle, and they loved to parade their virtue and wisdom and knowledge around in public.

We all know people like this, don't we? Their sharp tongues push snapshots of Jesus that make Him look judgmental. Their holier-than-thou attitudes give God a bad name. But you know what? Back in His day, Jesus wasn't having it. Wherever He went, He confronted the hypocrites.

The story is told in John 8:1-11. (Most of the earliest New Testament manuscripts do not include John 7:53–8:11. But the passage is in my Bible, so I'm going with it!) The scribes and Pharisees discovered a woman having sex with someone else's husband. My whole body gets tense when I think of the whole scene and how they didn't pull the scoundrel man along with her when they shoved the woman into the spotlight. No doubt she wasn't wearing much. Did they enjoy that?

The main goal that day was to trip up Jesus, but they didn't mind humiliating this woman and building up their egos along the way. If it happened today, think of the pictures that would be going viral on social media, with hashtags of brutal name-calling and inciting comments of both glory and shame.

After reminding Jesus that Moses's law said they should stone the woman, the surly crowd asked Him what He thought they should do. Then they stood waiting for a response.

Jesus seemed to be preoccupied drawing in the sand. I don't usually lean toward passive-aggressive moves, but I can't help but smile when I read this text.

> They made her stand before the group and said to Jesus, "Teacher, this woman was caught in the act of adultery. In the Law Moses commanded us to stone such women. Now what do you say?" They were using this question as a trap, in order to have a basis for accusing him.
>
> But Jesus bent down and started to write on the ground with his finger. When they kept on questioning him, he straightened up and said to them, "Let any one of you who is without sin be the first to throw a stone." . . .
>
> [Later] Jesus asked her, "Woman, where are they? Has no one condemned you?"
>
> "No one, sir," she said.
>
> "Then neither do I condemn you," Jesus declared. "Go now and leave your life of sin." (John 8:3-7, 10-11)

Jesus justifiably could have been the first one to throw a stone, right? But He didn't. He didn't use the sin of another to promote His own righteousness. He had another message.

If you want to have a voice that champions others, seek to offer seeds of help, not stones, when someone is hurting. We don't have to be geniuses to find flaws and point out sins in the people we interact with—at least not in my house. Exposing another person's problem isn't going to be all that helpful for them, but speaking to the nature of who they actually are and what they're capable of will help silence the voice of accusation.

Lives can get messy. We don't know all the reasons why we do the things we do or why we lean toward certain sin and proclivities. But Jesus isn't afraid to get close and speak to what needs to be helped. His words not only saved the woman from stones, but when He spoke to her pain, I'm guessing it changed her path.

Our words can be as weighty as rocks. I pray we use them in a way that lands gently in the hearts of others.

SOIL & SEEDS

In one of His parables, Jesus used a great analogy involving words, seeds, and soils. He was speaking about the things that steal from our hearts and how we either receive or stop His word from taking root when it is thrown into our lives. The story is told in Matthew 13.

Jesus later explains to His followers that "the seed falling on good soil refers to someone who hears the word and understands it. This is the one who produces a crop, yielding a hundred, sixty or thirty times what was sown" (Matthew 13:23).

I believe that our words, like His, can have the same effect. When we speak, we are ultimately scattering our words onto the soil in the hearts around us.

Some hearts will have a prepared soil, ready to receive. Some will be hardened, having no place for our words to land, much less take root. However, the job of the farmer in this parable is not to prepare the soil but only to think about the seed that is to be scattered. That may seem backward. What farmer would plant something before he readied the soil? In this analogy, though, the farmer's only role is to throw the seed. (I may be jumping to conclusions, but I'm thinking that if he wants to see a lot of growth around him without first attending to the soil, then he will need to be very generous with the seed he scatters, right?)

When you work to sow praise, truth, and encouragement and extend yourself in any way, remember that it's not your problem if that word isn't received. It is the problem of the owner of the soil. You can't weigh the strength of your words or your next steps by how people react to you. Just scatter wherever God has you as you extend heaven's heart. I've felt uncomfortable plenty, been embarrassed about having to do something I didn't want to do, but because I have resigned to be a partner with God, I try not to ever hold back.

Sometimes scattering goes well, and sometimes it doesn't. I've given words to people at grocery stores, asked if I could pray for someone at the mall, taken the shoes off my feet to give to the barefoot lady standing outside in the cold at a gas station (but I have to admit, I held onto my new denim jacket, which I should have offered too). I've brought chocolate chip cookies, a little overbaked, to a friend when I forgot to buy a gift after she had her fourth child.

We can't wait to throw seed until people are applauding. Eventually their hands will get tired, and they will stop. Then you will have to decide for yourself what your motive is. If we worry about getting critiqued or criticized, we will miss what God is up to in that moment. All kinds of things can go wrong when we try to offer hope and extend our love; good thing we are measured by our obedience as loved children and not by what we got right or what went wrong.

Scattering seed—in other words, throwing confetti—is about willingness, not giftedness. Some of us will never get off the couch if we think we've got to get everything all right. If we move ahead to do the things God is asking and step into what He's prioritizing, then we can rest easy because, like the farmer in Matthew 13, we've done our part.

BIT BY BIT

My father-in-law was an old soul. We always said Jon was born at least a hundred years after his time. He didn't own farmland, but the overalls he constantly wore would make you think he did. He harnessed honey from local honeybees, tended to a huge organic garden, and kept a set of draft horses—inside the city limits. He was an original, to say the least, with a very generous heart.

One day my mother-in-law came home from work and saw him being dragged down the middle of the street by his draft horses. They may have been beautiful creatures, but this situation was less than ideal. What a sight! I don't know if the bit was loose or what, but Jon had no way to steer them. So he opted to hang on for dear life while they proceeded to drag him down the middle of the street. No permanent damage was done, but the dangers of a loose bit proved to be quite terrifying.

James, the brother of Jesus, writes in his letter about the power of our words. He uses at least one analogy my father-in-law would recognize.

> When we put bits into the mouths of horses to make them obey us, we can turn the whole animal. Or take ships as an example. Although they are so large and are driven by strong winds, they are steered by a very small rudder wherever the pilot wants to go. Likewise, the tongue is a small part of the body, but it makes great boasts. Consider what a great forest is set on fire by a small spark. The tongue also is a fire, a world of evil among the parts of the body. It

corrupts the whole body, sets the whole course of one's life
on fire, and is itself set on fire by hell. (James 3:3-6)

It's clear that you and I don't have to use a lot of words to make
waves or create smoke. That's why we must guard our words
continually. What we say is an overflow of what's inside. If we
say things that hurt people, we need to honestly look at what's
hurting us. Upholding *hooray* is about extending the right words
at the right time.

> For the mouth speaks what the heart is full of
> (Matthew 12:34).

It's using our mouths to bless so we can make people's lives brighter,
not dimmer. That can mean confronting something, encouraging
someone, making apologies, and sometimes just sitting in silence.

If we don't know what the situation calls for, we can just ask.
James has words for that too.

> If any of you lacks wisdom, you should ask God, who gives
> generously to all without finding fault, and it will be given to
> you. (James 1:5)

When we posture ourselves in a way to hear from God, then we
can know how to best extend *hooray* in any moment. The Apostle Paul teaches that God revealed His truths to him through the
Spirit, "since the Spirit searches everything, even the depths of
God" (1 Corinthians 2:10 CSB). As followers of Christ, you and I
are fortunate enough to, through the Spirit, be able to have "the
mind of Christ" (1 Corinthians 2:16)—and therefore have the
breath of His words as well.

GETTING PRACTICAL

Our nonprofit, Refuge, got started not by some well-thought-out plan but sort of by accident. Brian would invite some friends to fish with him, friends who happened to be doing the same kind of Kingdom work he was doing. When the week would be over, the men would be smiling as new life was restored within them. They'd feel energized and hopeful. They had been reminded of important things by the God Who loved and first called them, and they again were excited about what they did. They returned home happy, which made their families happy and their staff happy.

Watching this happen over and over, Brian and I started intentionally learning about sabbath, rest, and the magnitude of burnout in Christian leadership. We started wondering who would be there to lead our kids and our churches if we didn't do something now about the statistics we were seeing.

Summer after summer these guys would invite more guys. Important conversations would be had, meaningful connections would be made, and once again our savings account would be drained. We knew at some point we'd have to turn this extracurricular confetti throwing into a nonprofit because the need was great and the cost kept climbing. We could barely keep up.

We gathered volunteers who turned into staff, bought a property, bought another property, and then made a life in the middle of nowhere so that men and women could come and escape to a sacred place—a refuge in which to be cared for.

Every week, we make at least a hundred hard decisions about what it means to share, give, extend, care, suffer, and love so that others can come to us without the daily pressures of what they carry and have time to sift through their own hearts. They take time to reflect from a different angle about all that life holds. Sometimes it's staff problems or personal traumas that need sorting through. Sometimes they just come to find inspiration and respite. They sit and contemplate what kind of wine should be poured for the evening and what cigar should be smoked. There just needs to be space for all of life's important matters to take a pause as we press into peace.

It was just one step for us, then another, then the next one. It was messy at times. It still is most of the time! But messy or not, these have been the right steps for us. It's how we throw confetti, and it's how our hearts practice *hooray* on a daily basis.

Everyone's expression of confetti looks different. Partnering with God will mean we have to make hard choices, but the shine it leaves behind and the dent it makes in the Kingdom are worth it.

I have dear friends who wanted to see God move in a big way in our city. They prayed for revival and gathered people for corporate prayer and worship. My girlfriend was a very supportive wife as her husband quit his well-paying, people-applauding job so that he could walk the streets in prayer. They sold their house, and she became the family's sole supporter as they sorted through what God might have them be doing.

They invited others to be a part of something new and unusual in hopes that the Spirit of God would "rend the heavens and come down" (Isaiah 64:1). It happened, too. People gathered monthly who wouldn't normally gather. People from different denominations, ethnic backgrounds, and theologies sat united in seats next to one another and called on God together. Our city had more compassion, and people had more support for one another. Ears were opened to hear what God was doing because my friends extended themselves and sacrificed to take a step, then another and another.

Another set of friends, Brittany and her husband, Sammy, run a "her-refuge" organization for victims of human trafficking. The amount of sorting through messes and baggage would overwhelm most of us. It's a good work with a whole lot of mess involved. I guess that's why the people of God are called to such works. We should be the ones who not only have pom-poms ready to cheer but our hands free to help. We've got to be willing to get dirty as we sift through the mud, ache, and pain with people.

Our friends in San Diego used to gather in a park to play games and eat food on Saturdays so that they could begin to engage their homeless community through play and fun. The invitation to fun seems rare these days, yet it's like a can opener to the heart that helps people receive who otherwise wouldn't.

Brian and I followed in their footsteps when we opened and ran a coffee shop (before Refuge grew to be full time). We'd gather some people on Friday nights and pass out coffee to our homeless community downtown. We'd offer warmth through a good cup, a prayer if they were open to it, or a ride, if they needed one.

It was our way of cheering and offering hope to some hurting people who rarely feel seen. More than once Brian and others got caught in some crazy situations. When you decide to throw confetti, you can't always predict how it is going to land. You can hope, you can guess, but you can't always know.

I guess if you like predictability, then you need to stick to numbers. Just about everything else is going to involve risk and create a mess while we look for the path. Find people to take steps with; they will make the journey so much better.

I realize that some type A personalities and Enneagram 1s are probably freaking out a little bit. I'm open to the idea that confetti works better when it is well thought through or at least prayed through and within our gifting. But honestly, sometimes we just have to start moving toward people and serving them as best we can. If we wait to get everything perfect, we might not ever do anything—and there is just so much to be done.

There are things that need to be said, hope that needs to be shared, apologies that need to be made, people who need to be restored. I think at some point we should just go for it. We start swinging, start scattering, and then see what happens and who comes along while the confetti is taking shape. We take a step and then watch the way forward that's being cleared for our next step. Soon the steps become clearer and a little easier to take.

YOUR PART

I could name leader after leader, group after group, and organization after organization we know doing a really good, really hard, and really messy work. We need more people in our world doing a good, hard, messy work.

We need more prison ministries, more water wells, more orphanages, and more help to those who are hurting. We need the things God has put inside each of us to be brought forward and extended. What you have to offer is greater than you realize. God doesn't need much to be able to multiply it.

There also is this: God will deposit something within us before others can get a glimpse of it. So it's normal if you can't see it yet or people can't speak to it. Who would have pictured a crown on the head of a baby in a messy manger? God loves to use unexpected people and unrealistic circumstances to show off what He is capable of doing with a life surrendered for His using.

God is calling you to something right now. He's calling us all into something for our future. "The one who has ears to hear, let him hear" (Matthew 11:15 NASB). What is it that you want Him to do for and through you?

Meditation

We're all a little messy at times. Remember that your voice is unique, your love is a reflection, and your life is needed. So please do not hold back!

So with that in mind, let's ponder some thoughts:
- How can you throw some confetti today?
- What are the passions, gifts, and talents God has given you to put to use?

REFLECTION

"The only thing that counts is faith expressing itself through love." (Galatians 5:6)

8

Standing Next to Strength

We were born to manifest the glory of God that is within us.
It's not just in some of us, it's in everyone.

—Marianne Williamson

GETTING STRONG

My sister used to work at a gym as a personal trainer. A while back I decided to take advantage of her services, hoping to lose "that last little bit" that never seems to fall off. I like to lean on the insight, talent, and experience of others. But I learned quickly that just because you stand next to someone with muscle, be it internal or external, that does not mean you'll gain any just from proximity.

One of a trainer's first steps is to take accurate measurements of you. That way they can create the right strengthening strategy as well as assess improvements. But a measuring tool is only for your development. It's not intended for you to use it to compare yourself to others, or to fill up your own head with judgments of others. (That might give you a fat head, which only adds to the weight that brought you to the gym in the first place!) Scales are great for baking and measuring sticks are useful for building, but should we take those tools and prop them up with the people around us, then they will only hinder us.

Comparing has a way of making us forfeit our *hooray*. We usually have to drop the megaphone to hold up the ruler. No one wants some Rambo beside them, determining how good they are based on someone else's performance. We should leave that kind of silliness to the toddlers in the daycare room. We don't want any limits on our ability to celebrate the "muscle" that others have grown and developed around us. Comparison will only compromise your cheer, so let go of any measuring you've been doing and get comfortable flexing the strength you have.

I love how Marianne Williamson puts it in her book *A Return to Love: Reflections on the Principles of a Course in Miracles*:

> Our deepest fear is not that we are inadequate. Our deepest fear is that we are powerful beyond measure. It is our light, not our darkness, that most frightens us. We ask ourselves, Who am I to be brilliant, gorgeous, talented, fabulous? Actually, who are you *not* to be? You are a child of God. Your playing small doesn't serve the world. There's nothing enlightened about shrinking so that other people won't feel insecure around you. We were born to make manifest the glory of God that is within us. It's not just in some of us; it's in everyone. And as we let our own light shine, we unconsciously give other people permission to do the same. As we're liberated from our own fear, our presence automatically liberates others.[2]

Perhaps the inclination to compare isn't so much about us not measuring up, but more about us feeling disappointed by our holding back when we know we are capable of more. When we acknowledge the strength and glory in another, there is almost an immediate heart scan that occurs within ourselves. If we let our inner critic evaluate the scan and not the Spirit, then we are going to feel diminished when we are next to such people. However, when we let the Spirit speak to our strength, when we stop shrinking and start shining, when we acknowledge the gifts of God within us, then we can be at rest with ourselves and cheer for others well.

I will tell you that I lost exactly zero pounds while my sister "trained" me, through no fault of hers. I liked the idea of a trainer more than I enjoyed someone telling me to lift heavier kettlebells or hold my position for longer than my legs wanted to support me. I continued to go to the gym, though, and she looked past my swearing and kept calling me to do more.

We build strength when we stand next to people. A lack of submission and teachability will keep us comfortable, but it will never stretch us in ways that we need it to.

We grow and develop based on what we do with the instruction that's given to us. If we don't allow other "trainers"—be it our Bible, mentors, our experiences, and so forth—to put some muscle on us, then our applause for others will be stunted. We have to "work out" and work at cheering and championing others until one day *hooray* feels like a lifestyle and not just something we do a couple times a month.

If we want to be open to all God has for us, then it's crucial we submit to His technique and strategy for our lives, no matter how hard the weight feels at times. Open heart, open hands, open mind, just open to what He shows us and who He puts in front of us, because even in the midst of social distancing, don't we still want to be as close as we can? It makes me think of when Mary, the mother of Jesus, finds just what she needs by visiting a friend.

STAND CLOSE

When Mary was just a girl, she had a "middle of the night" visit from an angel, which of course is a story in itself. In the Bible, angels don't show up without reason. They come with announcements, commands, insight, and directions. For this young daughter, the angel came as the spokesperson of God, announcing that she was highly favored and would be giving birth to the Savior of the world.

Now, if you still think Christmas is about getting your favorite things wrapped up and put under a tree, or if you're investigating your faith and the claims of Jesus, or if you struggle with believing the miraculous, this claim is a lot to swallow. Yet, those were the words Mary tucked into her heart and tried to get her head around as she went off to visit her older relative, who was perhaps a cousin, looking for comfort. Here's the text.

> Mary set out and hurried to a town in the hill country of Judah where she entered Zechariah's house and greeted Elizabeth. When Elizabeth heard Mary's greeting, the baby leaped inside her, and Elizabeth was filled with the Holy Spirit. Then she exclaimed with a loud cry, "Blessed are you among women, and your child will be blessed! How could this happen to me, that the mother of my Lord should come to me? For you see, when the sound of your greeting reached my ears, the baby leaped for joy inside me. Blessed is she who has believed that the Lord would fulfill what he has spoken to her!" (Luke 1:39-45 CSB)

Who we choose to share our words and promises with is of huge importance. It was risky for Mary to tell anyone that the God of the universe was going to supernaturally get her pregnant. But how would you ever keep that to yourself? The response of Elizabeth is worth remembering the next time a loved one comes to you looking for support. Elizabeth's words had the power to put Mary into a tailspin if she had responded by hammering her with "how could this be?" kind of questions. Her reply had the power to cast doubt, usher in fear, or cause Mary to reject the importance of her experience. Instead her words brought hope and confirmation; they were filled with wonder and celebration and were in agreement with what God said.

Elizabeth's feedback extended to Mary the freedom to dream, hope, cherish, and treasure the promised word within her. Her words of *hooray* landed safely in a heart that needed confetti and not criticism about all that God could be up to.

It's equally important when we get a word from God that is life-changing for ourselves or for others should we birth it to fruition, that we be careful who we take it to. Consider the context of the person you want to share this word with while you make room for God's word to grow within you.

Mary had the sweet privilege to share the gift of birth with a trusted family member and companion who could celebrate what God was doing. When God chooses to speak, His words must be protected and fostered with care at conception. It can be a delicate matter to believe such kind and gracious words about our future, and not everyone can handle them with cheer and champion us through the process without jealousy, comparison, or frustration.

Interestingly enough, it was the angel who first suggested to Mary that she might "consider your relative Elizabeth" and what God had done for her, saying "nothing will be impossible with God" (Luke 1:36-37 CSB). I love that God was the one directing Elizabeth to be the source of strength for Mary. He knows we need others to lean on, and I find it so kind of God to allow these two women to share their journey with one another. Mary needed a friend, and she needed to find strength for her days ahead. No doubt Elizabeth's words would echo in her heart through the many months and years ahead.

DON'T LET GO

When we rush to share God's Voice with those who don't have the capacity to celebrate what He's doing—which, of course, is a good goal—I wonder if there's fallout. I'm thinking of how often we might be ignoring or dropping or mishandling the prophetic promises and words of hope that God gives us.

We may be approaching the wrong person. Maybe we're holding back for some reason. We may simply be forgetting God's words spoken over us.

Isaiah 43:26 calls for us to "review the past." That means we are to remind ourselves and give thought toward the things God has told us. This practice develops an expectation in us and keeps us pressing in through prayer until we see our promises through to their fulfillment.

I'd say it's as important as looking at our bank statements. We need to know the deposits that have been made so we can better manage our transactions. When we can't recall the things the Spirit of God has said, it can put us at a deficit and move us toward a negative balance in our spirits. The only way to get out of that hole is with more deposits and fresh reminders. Friends have a way of reminding us of God's promises and of adding faith to our hearts as they stir up hope for all God can do. And plenty of visits with the Lender won't hurt either!

The Lender is looking to make a return on the things He's saying to us. His words may be commodities of great worth, but they are not given to us just to stay locked up in our hearts. They're intended to be used like wealth for the advancement of His Kingdom.

God will never run out of resources. There is no shortage of things He wants to say. So if you find yourself to be out of balance or in the negative when it comes to His words for you, then take some time to be with Jesus and ask the Spirit to speak so you can start to build your account back up.

To switch to a different metaphor, I believe that God gives us words with the intention that as we carry them, they grow in us until they are birthed. Granted, the birthing process is rarely clean or easy; it's why we need friends to hold our hand, doulas to remind us to breathe, and midwives to coach us on our technique—assuring us that it will all be okay.

We have to labor to see God-sized things come into fruition in our lives. We have to go through the birth pains, wade through the Braxton Hicks moments, and then push with endurance to see the birth of something new. And who knows, maybe a little like Mary, some of us will birth something that will change things for generations to come.

THE GREATER FRIEND

We all need people next to us who, in spite of our shortcomings, love us fully. Not just love our strengths but love all of us: our weaknesses, shortcomings, failures, and quirks. When these great people are near, keep them close! Anyone who cheers for the entirety of who we are is a gift from God.

At the same time, as much as we want other people to be great for us, we must be great for them too: great cheerleaders, great supporters, great friends. Great at forgiving, but not great at holding grudges. Great at letting go, but not great at clinging when we know it's time to say farewell. Great at vulnerability and authenticity, but not great at keeping our distance so others don't know how imperfect we are.

We don't become great at loving and cheering all on our own; we need help and plenty of it. Our kids don't become great without us fostering and facilitating their hearts. And as grown-up kids ourselves we still need the transforming work of Christ to help shape and fine-tune us. Oh yes, we can be great at a lot of things, but what if we got really great at unlocking our loving and our cheering?

Lately, instead of *me* trying to be great at anything, I've started asking God to become *greater in me*. I've been praying this simple prayer. Maybe you'd like to consider praying something like it.

> *God, be great at helping me let go of anything hindering my love. God, be great at opening my eyes to see the gifts and beauty in others.*

*God, be great at helping my hands create something beautiful
that I am not fully capable of on my own.
God, be great at showing me opportunities to care for others
that I might miss on my own.
God, be greater in me that it might draw others to You.*

LOVING OTHERS AS . . .

There are few things more wonderful than a trusted friend, and that's the opener for the next story we're going to look at involving friendship, loyalty, and an applause that outlasts a lifetime.

Two guys named Jonathan and David become unlikely but deeply bonded friends in the midst of tumultuous family dynamics. David was raised as a shepherd; Jonathan was a prince. Their story unfolds like a *Dateline* episode. Jonathan's dad was King Saul, who grew increasingly jealous of David, even to the point of trying to have him killed on several occasions. The repercussions of these men not getting along would change history for not just one kingship but the entire nation.

That's not what we're focusing on right now, though. We want to look at the amazing friendship of Jonathan and David. We see the first expression of Jonathan's heart toward David in 1 Samuel 18. The first and third verses read,

> When David had finished speaking with Saul, Jonathan was bound to David in close friendship, and loved him as much as he loved himself. . . . Jonathan made a covenant with David because he loved him as much as himself. (csb)

There is no deeper bond than that, is there? Now jump down to 1 Samuel 18:4.

> Then Jonathan removed the robe he was wearing and gave it to David, along with his military tunic, his sword, his bow, and his belt. (csb)

By all accounts Jonathan, even more than his father Saul, should have been threatened by David. Even though David wasn't after it, Jonathan's crown was on the line. It was David who had killed the giant, Goliath. It was David who could play the harp so well that it soothed Saul's troubled soul in the temple courts (see 1 Samuel 16:14-23). It was David who roused the songs of the city when he walked by (see 1 Samuel 18:6-7). And it would be David who would lead the army of Israel more successfully than any other commander.

Yes, from the outside, Jonathan had plenty of cause to be concerned. Yet he gave David his royal robe, his military tunic and belt, and his sword and bow. This act moved the friendship past mutual respect and enjoyment into the realm of divine connection.

Jonathan's eye wasn't measuring up David. He was filled with love and admiration. When we choose to view others through truth and not a lens of jealousy, we can see them for the gifts that they are. Jealousy doesn't allow us to see the whole picture of someone. It's like our eyes are squinting and blurry. *Hooray*, on the other hand, has eyes wide open, recognizing the beauty and imploring the strength inside of someone.

It's simple math. We want to bring addition to people, not division or subtraction. Jonathan added to David's life. He added to his heart, added to his wardrobe, and added to his leadership.

Adding to the lives of our friends doesn't mean we need to subtract from ourselves. But as Jonathan demonstrated, sometimes it is necessary. The removal of Jonathan's robe was not only a generous gesture but a prophetic act, indicating that though Jonathan was in line for the throne, it was going to be David who would sit on and rule from it.

What a treasure Jonathan was to David. When our love is extravagant, we will give expressively. When you find a friend like Jonathan, whose words are well matched with their actions, hold on because that kind of loyalty and integrity is a formula for something deep and meaningful.

Here's what I've found after reading these insightful and hard-to-swallow verses. It's easier for me to want and hope and pray for that kind of friend than to actually be one sometimes. Anyone? We like our robes and the things that protect us. We can get accustomed to the places we stand and thereby not take a fond liking to anyone who seemingly tries to "cut in front of us."

Fitting others for the things that feel good on me—gulp!—that's hard to choke down even on a good day. But we'll never throw confetti with that posture. *Hooray* will die before it has a chance to grow if we keep our fists locked, our lips pursed, and the walls up protecting our hearts where no one can ever get close enough to be cared for.

Our inner circles should be about giving and receiving, about being loved and loving on. So keep clapping for the people who need to receive, but like Jonathan, stay close to the ones God has anointed you to be next to.

. . . AS YOURSELF

What main thought did you take away from the story of Jonathan and David? Over and over I hear that mantra: "He loved him as much as he loved himself."

But here's a follow-up question: Is applying that standard to our lives a relief—as in "Oh, I can do that . . ."—or a challenge we don't always meet?

I guess the answer depends on how much we love ourselves. How much we know our value in God's eyes and look after our personal well-being is a good indicator of the length we'll go to see that another person gets as much love, care, help, and support as we would expect.

It's a serious matter. Jesus Himself echoed our Jonathan mantra when someone asked Him to name the most important command from God. He listed two, and the second was "love your neighbor as yourself" (Mark 12:31).

This kind of love is not only a command, it's a sign to the world.

> I give you a new command: Love one another. Just as I have loved you, you are also to love one another. By this everyone will know that you are my disciples, if you love one another. (John 13:34-35 CSB)

How well we're meeting the challenge these days is open to debate. Right or wrong, lots of folks in our culture hear the term *Christian* and think "hypocrite" or "narrow-minded" or worse. The Church has some work to do.

Practicing *hooray* is going to hurt sometimes. At least it does in my life, for several reasons. There is a whole heap of pride, ego, selfishness, and wrong motives I must wade through before I can love others well and find something meaningful to extend to them. Only then, if I say something, it's not just my voice sounding good and my exterior looking good; my heart means good too.

This is the invitation that calls me back to the wrestling mat with *hooray*. I'm always rooting for *hooray* to win in my life. But to be honest, my flesh is a good fighter, and I'm also trying hard not to let *hooray* hold me to the ground for too long. It's a struggle and a refining process. Often painful, but always worth it.

When my back is pinned to the ground, it only gives me one angle. I have to look up. Eyes up, heart up, and face toward the heavens with one message to receive: there is a purpose much bigger than me to live for.

Letting go of our lives so that others can benefit is a central theme of the gospel. It is part of the Jonathan mantra; it is part of the second great commandment. It is the anthem that Jesus walked and taught. It is the message He commissioned us to carry, and the banner He raised as He made His way up the hill dragging His cross on His back.

Crosses are heavy, and the weight is painful. We are always going to need others to help us carry burdens. Jesus Himself accepted strength from Simon of Cyrene (see Luke 23:26), who helped bear His weight so that He could make it to Calvary and fulfill His mission.

It's actually how we fulfill the law of Christ, which is the law of love.

> Carry one another's burdens; in this way you will fulfill the law of Christ. (Galatians 6:2 CSB)

BEARING BURDENS

Thinking about that scene of Jesus's road to Calvary brought up a lot of things. Here was Jesus, stripped of His clothes, beaten and whipped to the edge of death, mocked, spit upon, and forced to carry His own cross up to Golgotha. Along the way, crowds of people watched.

Maybe some spectators on the side of the ruling elite were cheering, like it was a Fourth of July parade. Maybe some were too stunned by the horror and injustice and felt powerless and paralyzed. Maybe some were moved enough to want to help but were too scared of the Romans to offer.

Is all that better than just looking away? Perhaps they tried to cheer Jesus a bit. Perhaps they snuck in an encouraging word. Perhaps they asked questions later, especially after they heard what happened in three days. But I think it's true of us that it's easier to watch a person struggle than to step in and help.

It's honorable to applaud and give encouragement with our voices as we see another doing a good work, but it's another thing entirely when we move from spectating and smiling to helping to bear a burden. When we help take on the weight of another, then we are loving them and thus fulfilling the law of Christ.

When we help shoulder something for others with the gifts God gave us and take weight off them, we have enacted a sincere love and fulfilled a supernatural purpose.

When people aren't weighed down by heavy burdens, their mission, messages, ministries, marriages (and the list goes on) can really soar. It's hard to fly when our hands are full. We need the momentum of other people to lift and carry us along.

WHAT'S LITTLE IN OUR LIVES?

There is not just a "certain kind of person" that needs to be helped. We all need help, and help comes in all kinds of different ways. Sometimes the "helpers" are the ones who are desperately in need of being helped. Some of us love being lenders but get really uncomfortable when it's our turn to receive.

I wonder if at some point this week you might exercise your asking as you would your offering. Ask for something that you need help with. Ask God for what you need increase on, ask a friend for help, ask a child, just start asking and see what might happen. Don't think about rejection; don't worry about how you are "putting someone out." Stop running through the reasons of why you think no one has the time or energy to help you and just let someone take some weight off you today.

On the flip side, say yes to the person at the grocery store when they ask if you need help loading your car, even if it's uncomfortable for you. Let your kids load the dishwasher even if you know they are gonna do it wrong. Ask your friend for the clothes in her closet that she never wears. Is that too far?

Love yourself well and ask for help. Let others love you well and let them help. Whether you're the one helping or being helped, maybe you will find that just like the boy with his backpack full of loaves and fish, you have even more than you did at first. More love, more care, more hope. Maybe even more generosity because you're not the only one giving all the time.

Let yourself get comfortable being the recipient of someone else's strength. God puts things within each of us to bless others; maybe it's your turn to be the recipient.

SHAKING & STRENGTHENING

I was flying home from a conference with some friends a while back, and luckily the Lord had favored me greatly and I got to sit next to my friend Dawn, who loves to fly. She has a lot of other great qualities and confetti is constantly in her pockets, but in this hour her greatest strength to me was her optimism about being in the air. She says it's because she "loves fair rides."

Just so you know, I don't mind fair rides either but I'm pretty aware that a roller coaster stays on the tracks as it spins around. When a plane begins to shake thousands of feet in the air while you are trapped inside, that feels more like a panic attack to me than "fun."

So there we were, thousands of feet in the sky, when the plane took on turbulence and all the signs came on to take your seat and stay buckled. I started my deep breathing, and then the next natural thing was to look for the flight attendant. I was trying to decide if she was faking her smile. Although her bright red lipstick was a nice distraction, it told me nothing about the predicament I felt we were all in.

The turbulence got worse. Now I was so close to tears I could barely keep them in. I turned toward Dawn and asked her if she *really* liked what was happening.

"Very much! It's just now getting fun," she said.

At that, I strangely felt some peace and I made myself reflect on a simple truth: it's nice to lean on another person's strength. I had nothing to offer Dawn in that moment, and that was okay because she didn't need anything from me.

Sometimes we will be the lender and other times the receiver, and we should get comfortable being both.

There have been countless other times that I have been the beneficiary of another person's strength, words, cheer, and presence that have brought me closer to the Father and have deposited confidence within me. Acting like I don't need someone's strength is not strong; it's weak. When we lack the acknowledgment that others have something great to offer, then our pride rises and our pom-poms fall.

Cheer is not something we want to let go of. There are plenty of other things that can be put down, like egos that don't leave any room to see what others carry, agendas that don't serve the greater good, and our own inner turmoil that seeks to suffocate our applause toward others. Planes are not the only things that cause turbulence in our lives. We get to be the people and we get to lean on the people who help steady us when things feel shaky.

Meditation

I hope you offer yourself today to those who need it, and I hope you ask for what you need without feeling bad about it. We are in a constant continuum of being helpers and getting to be the helped. Our strength is for others, and their strength is for us.

So with that in mind, let's ponder some thoughts:
- Is there anything you currently need help with this season? Who can you ask?
- Is there a way you can help another with their load this season?

REFLECTION

"One who loves a pure heart and who speaks with grace will have the king for a friend." (Proverbs 22:11)

Parts + Pieces + Practices

You can't go back and change the beginning,
but you can start where you are and
change the ending.

—Attributed to C. S. Lewis[3]

AN OCCASION FOR EVERYTHING

I have no patience for manual stuff, like putting together furniture. If I make progress and happen to leave a few parts on the floor, that's fine. I know it's not the most thorough job, but I tend to prefer speed over specifics.

Our plumber has a great sense of humor about this. I got to know him well because one winter we had no running water for three months due to our septic pipes freezing up. Let's just say my husband and I got through that ordeal by watching episodes of *The Office* on repeat while scrolling Zillow because our plumber's professional opinion was that only "time" could thaw this large piece of frozen piping. When that four-letter word came out of his mouth, it hit my ears like profanity.

Time can't be hurried, no matter how much we are in need of it. Things take time to unthaw and unfold. By the grace of God there aren't a lot of shortcuts to get us to where we're headed. Heaven help us if we get there too soon. Then, because of a lack of development on our part, we might not have the proper weight and girth of character to hold us up properly. Not everything can be handled like my throw-it-together furniture.

Every season of life can establish, develop, and grow something in us if we will partner with God and examine our hearts with the time we're given—and not wish it to thaw faster. There was a period when my kids were small and my mothering was consumed by chasing toddlers and wading through diapers that I felt like time had shrunk. A minute was a second, an hour a minute, a day an hour. Even though people told me it wouldn't be this way forever, I couldn't imagine a day when there would be space in my schedule where I had the time for more independence.

Our roles change with the different seasons we find ourselves in. We must be intentional about changing with the times in order to play our part. A wise king once wrote, "There is an occasion for everything, and a time for every activity under heaven" (Ecclesiastes 3:1 CSB).

If that's true, and I believe it is, then we need to be people who not only know what time it is, we also need to know what's needed from us with the time we have. Our parts will vary, and the pieces we contribute will naturally change and evolve. What part is ours to play, and what is our piece to contribute in this season?

PARTS

———

The Apostle Paul teaches us about all the wonderful parts in God's collective body of believers. He reminds us that diversity isn't only needed, it's essential to sustain balance and health.

> Indeed, the body is not one part but many. If the foot should say, "Because I'm not a hand, I don't belong to the body," it is not for that reason any less a part of the body. . . . If the whole body were an eye, where would the hearing be? If the whole body were an ear, where would the sense of smell be? But as it is, God has arranged each one of the parts in the body just as he wanted. And if they were all the same part, where would the body be? As it is, there are many parts, but one body. (1 Corinthians 12:14-15, 17-20 CSB)

I think the Christian community has lost sight of a couple things. First, we are all part of the same body, grafted together, working beside each other, under one purpose, in order to play a collective part.

Second, there are many parts. Different sets of eyes will see in various ways; different minds will have unique visions and original ideas. There are a lot of talented people out there, with all kinds of expressions that are needed to offer help and hope to others.

That gospel truth should rally our inner cheerleader and cause our *hoorays* to rise. It's important that each of us has the opportunity to align ourselves with the head which makes our heart beat and with the body that values the piece we have to contribute.

Each piece is essential. We are made in His perfect image, saved by the same blood that made us all free, and sent on a mission to serve the King and build His Kingdom.

If the body has a head but no hand to help accomplish something, or if it has no eyes to see, then what good is it for that head to keep giving directions? If the parts on the inside of our body that are not seen begin to shut down, it will affect the whole functioning of the body. The ways in which we are made and the gifts God puts in our hands aren't just for us. They are there to benefit those next to us. What we have is for a greater purpose and to be of benefit to the whole body.

There are so many roles we need to fill, parts we need to play, and gifts we need to use within God's body, the Church, that we don't want to waste time worrying about what we aren't. Let's just move ahead by stepping into what we are so we can accomplish bigger things together.

Does that take time? Yes, and it will need to unfold with intention. What are you good at? What are your dreams and desires? When you pray, are you an "ear," an "eye," or a "heart"? Do you see, hear, know, or feel? Our bodies' physical senses serve a metaphorical purpose too. The book of Hebrews talks about the spiritually mature "whose senses have been trained to distinguish between good and evil" (Hebrews 5:14 csb). When you sit next to other people or talk with your neighbor, do you feel, see, or know certain things as you are close to them?

We have gifts the Father gives us to help serve and *build up* the body. We are all responsible to discover and know them, grow them, hone them, and extend them. Just as gifts are given on birthdays or for other sweet reasons, our spiritual gifts are given by God as a present to us. Let's make sure that when we open our gifts, we don't just gawk at them and applaud them, but let's actually develop and use them as they are intended. Our gifts and talents are to be offered for the greater good and serve a purpose in the body so it functions well.

Third, let's celebrate what God is up to—down the road, down the hall, or just down the aisle. God is doing something different in every family, every church, every work site, and every heart because it's good. Different is good; unity doesn't mean uniformity. Let's make space for God to be as creative as He wants to be with us and those around us.

There are so many parts in the body, parts we can see and parts we don't even know exist, but we all know that the body moves best when all the parts are functioning in harmony. Let's move on from criticism and get ahold of celebration so we can keep in step with how Christ has asked us to live: "Let us consider how we may spur one another on toward love and good deeds" (Hebrews 10:24).

Spurring doesn't require our understanding. All too often our applause is stifled because we "don't get it." We don't need to always "get it" to be able to spur it on. People don't "get me" plenty and they're not going to always "get you," but if we can get past what we don't get and just try to get God's heart for them, then we can be thankful that a piece of the body is working even in ways we don't understand.

So for goodness' sake, *clap your hands*. God has given each of us the task of fanning the flame and standing in the cheering section with one another as we move toward love and good deeds. Let's do as Hebrews says and really consider how we may spur, urge, and propel others onward.

MORE PARTS

Each of us has something to contribute to each other. Each of us has a portion to give, because each of us is revealing a unique side of God. That uniqueness is manifested through our individual makeup as designed by God and expressed in our personality. We carry something different and special to the people around us.

God is eccentric and creative. Our personal uniqueness is flavored by our interpretation of who He is in our life and how we see Him. We learn a new side of Him as we take note of how others "flavor" the spaces they are in. Then we hear from Him and express Him differently with our own style and expression.

A good number of us have lost confidence in this, because we've gotten caught up in comparing ourselves to the styles of others. It keeps us from extending what we have.

Only you can extend what's inside of you in the way God intended it. Only you can bless, encourage, rally, champion, support, and speak to the people God has you around with the flavor that's been developed in your life because of your unique set of challenges, blessings, trials, and experiences.

When we don't show up and play our part, others miss an attribute of God that could bless them. They miss out on the portion that only we have to offer. That's why it's important that we extend to others in the places that God puts us.

Every player needs to stay in their sphere of influence, doing the very best they can, playing their part for the team. When they don't show up ready, when they haven't practiced, or when they get out of position, we have no one to pass to or receive from, and it's a loss for the whole team.

I played on a traveling soccer team with teammates who became quick friends. We learned the field and positions together, and over time it was easy to see and adapt to each other's talents and strengths. We knew how to maneuver and work together on the field and how to fill in the gaps for each other when positions were in transition.

In one tournament we were playing against a team, and we just couldn't find our groove. We weren't racking up any points on the scoreboard even though we were dominating their half of the field. Every pass felt like it was in slow motion, and we just couldn't find the back of the net. So Andy, our goalie, took it upon herself to leave her post and make a run at the other team. It was a mixture of frustration and boredom that made her abandon her position in the goal and leave us vulnerable.

I'm laughing as I recall the scene. The ball that felt more comfortable in her hands was now being scrambled around with her feet. It was pretty wild and reckless, but her actions did something to shift us into another gear. It's a cherished memory.

If we don't play our part, someone may come in and do it for us. Someone who might have a different set of skills, but enough leadership to know it's time to get something done.

There are so many churches, ministries, jobs, families, and schools in desperate need of people who will play their part. Sure, we might be able to get the job done by maneuvering others around and changing tactics. But teams perform best when everyone is playing the position that they have skills for. When we play the part we have been assigned to play, everyone benefits. We feel a part of something bigger, and we accomplish something together.

And by the way, you won't always feel "skilled" for the part you've been asked to play, even if you have the gifting for it. Roles can be learned; we can become students no matter what age we are and learn a new role in a new season if God should be calling for it.

I love this thought from Saint Irenaeus, sometimes translated like this: "The glory of God is man fully alive." When we bring all of who we are into the rooms we're in, then God is glorified. He's more known and more is revealed about who He is just by us being fully who we are.

Flavor the rooms you're in. Leave something of substance in the places you go. Don't be afraid to shine and be fully you so that others can see what a great Creator God is.

PARTNERSHIPS

I didn't run track for very long. I couldn't stay motivated to work at something all on my own. Individual sports are great, and watching others who are good at them has taught me something about perseverance and endurance. But I'm wired for partnerships.

I need someone to pass to and someone to receive from. I need others close when I'm about to go up against an opponent. It feels best when others are playing their part right beside me and not making measurements against me. I love knowing that if I've scored, it's because everyone else has done their part and played their position well. We can all celebrate together.

When it comes to strategy, positions, and partnerships, I believe the Kingdom of God works a little like a soccer field.

I have a prayer group that meets together regularly. We've prayed long enough beside each other to know how to navigate a room. We recognize how to hold a word and when to release what God is saying over another. We've learned how to maneuver and lean in to rely on each other's gifts and skills. One friend plays the role of intercessor, getting the room ready through prayer beforehand and creating space to open up all that God has in mind for those who will come to gather. Others of us get into position to hear the word of the Lord, to hear what is being said by the Spirit and how to best move forward. We all stay in position and practice how to see, hear, feel, and extend.

Scoring can't happen alone. It's dependent on everyone playing their part, staying in position, and having a partnership with the

Holy Spirit as our "coach." Since we all are given only a portion to carry, it's imperative we all participate to give what we have in order to see the whole picture, to make a collective sense of what God is up to.

We regularly see people come into the group with burdens and leave in freedom. They don't just leave feeling "nice"; they leave feeling free because the God Who spoke the world into existence long ago is still speaking today, building and creating things brand new. Nice won't help a devastated heart or a tormented soul. Thank goodness we can get before God and listen to our heavenly Coach, Who is actively imparting, talking, wooing, and pursuing us. He's releasing hope and truth to captives, freeing prisoners, restoring vision, and reminding us of how good He is.

Those prayer gatherings also are a good place to practice *hooray* and spread a little confetti around. We listen to people's stories and simultaneously ask the Father to cue us in to what He's up to. Then with their permission, we can extend what we may have heard.

My words alone don't have enough holding power to help someone. They are important, but to have lasting benefit for someone, we need God to breathe on what we're saying. That means we need to hear what He is saying so we can say it. Each of us has to get our souls and spirits quiet so that we can lean into what God has on His mind and in His heart for someone.

Most partnerships end up going well or breaking down, depending on how we are positioned and if we are listening. In the book of Job, it says, "A word was brought to me in secret; my ears caught a whisper of it" (Job 4:12 csb). I want to position myself in such a way that no whispers are getting missed.

RESURRECTED LIFE

I for one couldn't follow God if I didn't believe He was an active partner of ours.

I grew up in a nice church that taught me the rules of religion: when to stand up, sit down, take a knee, recite a verse, and how many Hail Marys to say after I did something bad. However, that good church forgot to teach me that though Jesus did a beautiful thing on the cross, He doesn't hang there still. I will add that my selfish teenage heart probably missed a ton of the important teachings. But looking back, it felt like a place that held onto the crucifixion of Friday and the death of Jesus, and never quite got around to the celebration of Sunday, the whole reason for our faith.

The resurrection is the whole reason that Christ came: not only to die, but to conquer. It's why we can expect to hear His whisper for ourselves and for others.

The resurrected God is bringing resurrected life to us in the form of whispers, words, and working power every single day, and thank goodness He is. I for one would be in a wretched state if this weren't the case.

> The Spirit of God, who raised Jesus from the dead, lives in you. (Romans 8:11 NLT)

Lives in you, lives in me, lives and moves and breathes and speaks!

GET READY

Countless stories in the Bible make it clear that how we position ourselves in relation to the Holy Spirit really matters. If we aren't leaning into the divine whisper, we won't know when to stay still and where to go next. I want to look at one such story. It involves a storm, a whisper, and a man who needed some help. I think it will give us more understanding on how to correctly posture ourselves.

In 1 Kings 18, there is a grand display going on, with wind blowing and fire roaring and chaos ensuing. Thankfully God elevates His whisper over all the commotion. In fact, I think His whisper seems all the more essential when there is a lot of noise around us.

Here's what happened. One of God's messengers, a prophet named Elijah, confronted a group of people who wanted nothing to do with the living God; they wanted instead to deal with the things they could control. So God did something major and miraculous to show Himself alive and present.

Elijah built an altar and gathered all the nation's false prophets (the Bible says there were 850 of them!). Then he challenged them to a duel of sorts. Prove the existence of their false gods by commanding them to send fire from heaven, and he would do the same. It was quite a showdown in front of all the people as well as the evil King Ahab and his even more evil wife, Jezebel.

After the bad guys prayed long and hard for an entire day, nada. Then Elijah said to step aside. He prayed to the Lord God, and bam! Fire rained down and burned up the altar!

A lot of hearts were turned to God that day because of Elijah's bravery and because of God's incredible working power. But the effort
took a toll on Elijah. Even though God came through and used
him as a vessel to show off Who God was, Elijah was spent. He was
more than spent; he was a wasted type of tired. That made him
vulnerable. Vulnerable to fear, to doubt, to giving up, and probably
to a handful of other things. And that's the time when the enemy
loves to go for the jugular, which is exactly what happened.

Jezebel, who loved her false prophets, was of course livid because
Elijah had had them all put to death. She started cursing Elijah
because his actions exposed her false hope.

> So Jezebel sent this message to Elijah: "May the gods strike
> me and even kill me if by this time tomorrow I have not
> killed you just as you killed them." (1 Kings 19:2 NLT)

Even though Elijah had just won an enormous battle proving
God was in fact alive and at work, he ran from Jezebel. Her scare
tactics were a bad mixture to be added to Elijah's burnout, and it
led him to ask God for a shortcut.

Collapsing in the wilderness, Elijah pleaded with the Lord.

> "I have had enough, LORD," he said. "Take my life."
> (1 Kings 19:4)

Have you ever been so tired from God's work, or so sick of fighting people in the midst of "ministry," that you'd rather just call
it quits? I think it's more common than some realize. Burnout
doesn't happen overnight; it's a slow fade of fight after fight after

fight. It becomes really dangerous when you, like Elijah, are the only one standing in the middle of the battles you're facing.

God answered Elijah in a sweet and somewhat surprising way—not with words, but with the comfort of something good to eat, delivered by an angel. Afterward He gave Elijah time for a nice long nap. God is so gracious to answer us in the ways that we need—not always in the ways that we want. Personally, I would have wanted words, but it's hard to hear God on the run when we are tired and scared.

So Elijah ate and then he slept, and after some rest, he was sent on a long journey, to Horeb, the mountain of God, also called Mount Sinai—where Moses received the Ten Commandments and experienced God passing by.

The morning after Elijah arrived, God came to him with an order.

> The LORD said, "Go out and stand on the mountain in the presence of the LORD, for the LORD is about to pass by." (1 Kings 19:11)

By this point our guy is open to hearing from God because exhaustion no longer has a hold on him. I find it interesting that God could have given Elijah any number of signs to reveal His presence and His activity, but His saving grace came to him in hushed tones.

> At that moment, the LORD passed by. A great and mighty wind was tearing at the mountains and was shattering cliffs before the LORD, but the LORD was not in the wind. After the wind there was an earthquake, but the LORD was not in

the earthquake. After the earthquake there was a fire, but the
LORD was not in the fire. And after the fire there was a voice,
a soft whisper. When Elijah heard it, he wrapped his face in
his mantle and went out and stood at the entrance of the cave.
(1 Kings 19:11-13 CSB)

The text says, "There was a voice, a soft whisper." And when Elijah heard that "voice, a soft whisper," he wrapped himself up and positioned himself to hear more.

Thank goodness Elijah didn't quit because he had a lot to teach us, as is shown in the pages of Scripture that follow. We are blessed recipients of his faith and prophetic ministry. I can't imagine what would have been lost had he run away from the part that was his to play.

The truth is that part of Elijah's saving grace was the whisper of God, and I believe part of ours will be the exact same thing.

PRACTICES

Certainly I'm not saying that every whisper is from God. We definitely need to be cautious about our own hearts and minds getting in the way of God's agenda and what He might want to say.

I like to practice daily the protocol from Jesus in Matthew 18:18. I simply bind up anything not congruent with God's way of thinking, and I loose the words of His heart to flow freely.

My next step is to ask the Holy Spirit to enlighten me and turn up the decibel of His speaking and working so that I don't miss what He's up to. I ask that my flesh and selfishness would be quiet and put in correct alignment under my spirit. I surrender my imagination to the Holy Spirit for His using, and I pray, as the Apostle Paul did, for "the Spirit of wisdom and revelation, so that [I] may know Him better" (Ephesians 1:17). Then I wait in expectation.

This is what often happens next: He gives me encouragement, warnings, ideas for the day, prayers to pray for those I love, and sometimes the necessary gift of silence. In addition, our kind and good God gives expression—through me—to someone He loves, through whispers, pictures, and thoughts that I couldn't have made up myself.

If the story of Elijah in 1 Kings 19 has taught us anything, it's that God's whisper has the ability to get us back on track and move us toward the next set of tracks. The beauty and authority of God's Word and His voice anchor our hope, assure our faith, and keep us coming back to Him for help, healing, and communion that His divine partnership makes possible.

DON'T MISS THIS PIECE

Our willingness will trump our giftedness, our talent, and even our intellect. When we are willing, God can use us and He will give us the grace that's needed to extend whatever we have.

In Exodus 3, God takes a man named Moses by surprise with an odd occurrence: a bush that's on fire. Curiosity can be a great first step toward willingness. When Moses moved to inspect the burning bush, God began to tell Moses what He wanted him to do, confirming His word to Moses through a sign.

Our experiences and encounters with God are significant markers for us. They oftentimes can be the glue that holds our faith together through the hard things we have to walk through when God is asking us to go.

When Moses heard His instructions, he responded by asking, "What if they do not believe me or listen to me and say, 'The LORD did not appear to you'?" (Exodus 4:1).

God asked him, "What is that in your hand?" (Exodus 4:2).

Moses was holding a staff, a pole with a hook on one end, used by shepherds to guide sheep. God told him to throw it on the ground.

> Moses threw it on the ground and it became a snake, and he ran from it. Then the LORD said to him, "Reach out your hand and take it by the tail." So Moses reached out and took

hold of the snake and it turned back into a staff in his hand. "This," said the LORD, "is so that they may believe that the LORD, the God of their fathers—the God of Abraham, the God of Isaac and the God of Jacob—has appeared to you." (Exodus 4:3-5)

God is still doing that with us, taking whatever is in our hands and in our hearts and moving on it with power in the moments we need help. Moses would use that same staff and those strong arms to lead a people through the sea and on to freedom. Who knows how long Moses would have stayed on the mountain, tucked in with all the sheep, if he hadn't had the willingness to do what God was asking? If he would have stayed stuck in his "what if" questions with the Lord, then his name might never be mentioned from our lips.

"What ifs" are important to process, important to think about, but they are of utmost importance to move *through*. Moses was a man scared to speak, scared to go, and scared he wasn't enough *amen*. Most of us can relate. But if we're not careful, the "what ifs" will suck the life right out of us until we are too paralyzed to move. "What ifs" will open the door to fear and failure, and if those thoughts aren't combated with new thoughts and God's thoughts, then possibly we will bow and mouths will be silenced.

If God has said to move, we must turn our "what ifs" into "willing ifs." I'm willing—if You'll go with me. I'm willing—if You'll show me. I'm willing—if You'll help me.

We need to take steps in the midst of our questioning and see what God will do. If not, the snake will have his way, and we will end up running instead of using what's in our hands.

I should mention that the rest of the story is a good one. God gave Moses a helper to go with him. For that I am thankful. The trend of doing ministry two by two continues throughout the New Testament (see Luke 10:1 and Mark 6:7). I don't think any of us are supposed to go alone at anything. Even in prayer Jesus says that where two or more are gathered together, He comes in our midst (see Matthew 18:20).

God's intention is partnership. The Trinity shows us that three isn't a crowd but a party, or at least a necessity. It's easy to get lost when we're by ourselves; we make more mistakes and become isolated, angry, and cynical. We can lose sight and lose heart. We need the megaphones of others reaching our ears, saying things like "please keep going," "we need what you have," and "I am with you."

The echoes of others are intended to sharpen us and put courage back inside us. We need every person with all their wild pieces playing the part that's meant for them. So please play your part; no one will do it better. You won't do it perfectly, and that's okay because you don't need to. All of us are navigating this puzzle together, trying to figure out just where we fit. We will try to squeeze, we will fail, and we will fall. And then we will get back up and try again because no puzzle is completed until all the pieces fit.

IT'S PART OF THE PUZZLE

It's not easy being in seasons when we don't feel like things are fitting. I'm not talking about pant sizes, though that's hard too, but the times in our life when we feel like we're just not sure if there's room at the table for us, for our gifts, or for the culture we carry with us.

I hate forcing puzzle pieces when I'm playing with my kids, but in real life, sometimes it's required. Eventually if it's not the right fit, the other pieces will force it out, or the pieces around it end up moving into place and adapting. The point is that we don't know unless we place our piece and see if it's a fit.

When Jesus sent out His boys to different towns, telling them to share the gospel, He certainly didn't say that they would fit in every place they went. In fact, it sounds as if He knew they wouldn't. "If people do not welcome you, leave their town and shake the dust off your feet as a testimony against them" (Luke 9:5). In other words, go and do something. If it's a fit and they receive you, that's wonderful, but if it's not a fit, just let it go and move on.

We try on spaces to see if they are a fit for us and to see how we can be useful there. But too often we think a bad fit is a failure. It's not a failure when we try to see how people, places, jobs, and cultures will work or not work for us. A bad fit is just a bad fit and a great opportunity to learn something. When we use all of our experiences as teachers and tools for ourselves, then we have all the more to offer others. We learn from not fitting as much as we learn and develop from a good fit. A good fit will keep us, but a bad fit will still grow us.

Meditation

So grow on with your bad fit, pray, and push through until God moves you. Let people see what a spirit of *hooray* looks like and what a gift you are to them as you play your part. If their eyes stay closed and they refuse to receive you, then just shake it off. The advice is not only a good pop song but a useful method from an ancient and living God helping us see our way through when we are refused. Shake it off, move along, and find out where you're going to fit next, because you do fit somewhere and we need your piece.

So with that in mind, let's ponder some thoughts:
- Where do you feel most comfortable using your gifts and expressing yourself?
- What "part" do you identify with in the body that Paul talks about in 1 Corinthians 12?
- How can you help "spur one another on toward love and good deeds" this week?

REFLECTION

"Just as our bodies have many parts and each part has a special function, so it is with Christ's body. We are many parts of one body, and we all belong to each other." (Romans 12:4-5 NLT)

10

Ruling & Reigning

The woman turned and went slowly into the house. As she passed the doors she turned and looked back. Grave and thoughtful was her glance, as she looked on the king with cool pity in her eyes. Very fair was her face, and her long hair was like a river of gold. Slender and tall she was in her white robe girt with silver; but strong she seemed and stern as steel, a daughter of kings.

—J. R. R. Tolkien, *The Two Towers*[4]

HOLY BOLDNESS

I am the oldest of three siblings. Birth order played in my favor. My sisters certainly wouldn't have willingly bent a knee for me, but I constantly (basically all of the time) used my position on top for selfish purposes, like threatening, "Go grab me this or else." Praise God I grew up, at least mostly, and my sisters didn't take revenge!

We all have unique places of influence that we need to consciously steward in order to make the most impact with those around us.

God needs only one person to spark a fire that will generate lasting heat for others. God needs only one voice that speaks with courage to shift change. Holy boldness is an option for all of us. I love stories of people like Rosa Parks, who lit a spark and got the nation's attention. On December 1, 1955, Rosa decided to be "holy bold" and chose to stay in her seat and not move to the back of the bus anymore. One act for the good of others can change a person, change a family, change society.

There is a voice in Scripture that I'm constantly drawn back to as I think about how one person's actions can forge a long-lasting legacy. A favored Jewish girl named Esther became a chosen queen, and because of her courage to step forward and speak up, a very jeopardized people kept their lives. Thousands of years after Queen Esther's rule, her story is still leaving pieces of confetti in my spirit.

WHEN THE KING CALLS

The story of Esther starts with a king. Many of the best stories do, but hold onto your hats: this tale is a doozy.

The Persian emperor Xerxes, known by his Hebrew name King Ahasuerus, had just thrown a six-month feast for his officials, staff, nobles, and provincial big shots, displaying "the magnificent splendor of his greatness" (Esther 1:4 CSB). Then he capped it off with seven days of banqueting and nonstop drinking.

> Drinks were served in an array of gold goblets, each with a different design. Royal wine flowed freely, according to the king's bounty. The drinking was according to royal decree: "There are no restrictions." The king had ordered every wine steward in his household to serve whatever each person wanted. (Esther 1:7-9 CSB)

What a first-class bender. Mental note: that's not the best time in which to upset a king, who back then had total power to do whatever he pleased.

Ahasuerus's wife, Queen Vashti, had thrown a parallel feast for the women of the palace. The empress was known for her beauty, and of course back then (and in some places still today!), she was virtually the king's property. Maybe she had gotten fed up with that and was in no mood to be paraded around just to stroke her hubby's gigantic ego; we aren't told. But what happened next sealed her fate.

On the seventh day, King Ahasuerus commanded some servants to bring Queen Vashti to his party, decked out with her royal crown.

> He wanted to show off her beauty to the people and the officials, because she was very beautiful. But Queen Vashti refused to come at the king's command . . . The king became furious and his anger burned within him. (Esther 1:11-12 CSB)

That's how the story of Esther starts: with a feud between a tipsy king and his beauty queen who made a regretful choice to stay back when she was called forward. Whatever Vashti's motive, her rebellion fueled fear in the men around her, who decided her stance would motivate all women, rich or poor, to take the same action when it came to obeying their own husbands!

So Ahasuerus consulted with his "experts in law and justice" (Esther 1:13 CSB) who advised him to banish Vashti forever from his presence, issue an order for women to honor their husbands, and find another queen. When fear is the dominant emotion, control usually follows. That is not a good combination. The queen played the wrong hand and ended up in handcuffs.

Women have had a long history of their voices being demoted, their motives attacked, and their vital roles downplayed. When people don't know how to handle strength, they can move to squelch it, if not completely cut ties to banish others. It's reasonable to remember that we should be careful when dealing with large egos. When the confetti isn't falling on them, watch out: it's a good bet they'll take measures to make sure *hooray* is loud for the one in charge. Queen Vashti did not learn that truth.

In contrast, let's remember that the King we serve doesn't seek to squelch our voices but wants to use them as a solution for redemption. The messages our voices carry become remedies for others; our words serve as salve to their wounds. So it seems of great importance that we would each learn how to move in the rhythms of timing, asking God which way to go and when.

When our King—obviously the opposite in temperament and motive from worldly Ahasuerus—calls you forward for something, don't hold your breath for long. If there is a seat He needs you to sit in, a stage He wants you to stand on, or a room that needs your voice, then it's best you step up. We are reading from the book of Esther and not the book of Vashti because timing *really* matters.

FAVOR

Once the search begins for a new queen, a young woman named Esther enters the king's palace, along with all the other women to be considered for the role of wife and influencer. We can't read the story of Esther and not pick up on favor. Time and time again she catches the attention of everyone in charge and makes her way toward the top.

> The young woman pleased [the keeper of women] and gained his favor so that he accelerated the process of the beauty treatments and the special diet that she received. He assigned seven hand-picked female servants to her from the palace and transferred her and her servants to the harem's best quarters. (Esther 2:9 CSB)

Favor is an interesting concept. It doesn't seem to be bestowed to us as freely as grace, love, or forgiveness. Those traits are part of an automatic inheritance we receive just for being kids of a King. And though we are all favored by God, we are not all favored by man. Esther, however, seemed to gain favor wherever she went. "Esther gained favor in the eyes of everyone who saw her"(Esther 2:15 CSB). To gain something implies that it can increase in our lives and that there is opportunity for us to obtain more of it. Scripture says about Jesus that He grew up into more favor: "And Jesus grew in wisdom and stature, and in favor with God and man" (Luke 2:52).

One of the ways to gain and grow in favor is by navigating the ways of the heart well. The Bible tells us that King David was chosen and anointed over all his older brothers "because the Lord doesn't look at the things people look at. People look at the outward appearance, but the Lord looks at the heart" (1 Samuel 16:7). What is not known to us is still known by God. So rest easy if you think you are being overlooked or you're just hoping to have a seat at the table; if God wants you somewhere, then He will get you there.

How we navigate and steward ourselves in private really matters to God. When I read through Scripture, I continually find that the shadows make great training ground for us. We are being trained all the time behind doors, behind people, and in places that no one else can see. We don't have to post about our situation to make it known to man, because it's known by God and He is the one bringing promotion and bestowing favor. "The eyes of the Lord are in every place, watching the evil and the good" (Proverbs 15:3 nasb).

There are plenty of verses like the one in Psalm 84 that make mention about what we have access to because of how we act. I'm not talking about ladder-climbing, but about knee-bending, about getting our hearts into the right position to be free of greed and selfish ambition. If our purity can lead the way and motivate the steps we take, then I think the amount of favor we can have will be insurmountable because nothing can stop a pure vessel from getting to where it needs to go. "The Lord bestows favor and honor; no good thing does he withhold from those whose walk is blameless" (Psalm 84:11). We don't do good acts in order to gain favor; we gain favor by doing good.

The key to Esther's ability to access favor comes down to her humility. We are told that she listened to the leaders in her life. She listened to her cousin (who was her legal guardian), and she listened to the eunuch who was placed over her. A heart that bends low and welcomes advice is just as the proverb claims: "To one who listens, valid criticism is like a gold earring" (Proverbs 25:12 NLT).

I'd suggest that much like two lovers, favor and humility keep close tabs on each other, because where humility walks, favor follows.

TIMING

I know some great listeners. I want to become a better one. My mind is usually on a trigger, ready to fire the next word. But sometimes what's needed is the quiet assurance and compassion of just being available. We'd be wise to start asking God, "Is this a time to be silent or a time to speak?"

Solomon, the wisest king ever to walk the earth, implied that we need to know what time it is. He taught that there is a time for everything, including silence. "There is a time for everything . . . a time to be silent and a time to speak" (Ecclesiastes 3:1, 7).

Good listeners rarely get enough credit for throwing confetti. Those who can sit in silence next to us while we are being heard are expressing a quiet *hooray* through their genuine expression of love. Confetti doesn't have to be loud or even be seen to be effective; it can just have a presence.

I think Esther must have been a listener. She listened to her cousin, Mordecai, who raised her (she was an orphan) and guided her toward saving her people. She listened to the servants in charge of the harem she had been assigned to and won the hearts of her attendants and eventually King Ahasuerus.

It was Esther's listening ear that motivated her response to act. Her listening activated her doing. We may hear people give us advice, but unless we listen deeply and adjust to the truth, we won't grow or change. Good listening leads to action, or else it's just a pleasant trait that leads nowhere.

Where it led Esther was into the throne room. God extended her favor and used her listening ear, a posture of humility, and a yearlong series of beauty preparations to win over the heart of the king. God bestows favor on purpose for a purpose. If we carry the favor of God, it will be because it's needed—not just for ourselves but, as we will soon see with Esther, for those He wants us to help. Our favor is ultimately for others.

We need favor to speak into the lives of others if we want to offer them hope, peace, and encouragement. We need favor when we go to those in positions of power to make requests. We need favor to light up dark rooms, neighborhoods, and workplaces so that we can shine God's love on the people He cherishes.

And as we do it in humility, it will open doors and make a way for us when we aren't sure where we are supposed to go next. The great thing about favor is that it's available to any of us. Keep your heart soft, hair trimmed, ears open, and knees flexed, and favor will track you down as it did Esther.

IT WAS ALL A SETUP

God is in the business of setting us up. Not in the sense of "for a fall," of course. More like a coach moving players into position so that someone can score. Or, perhaps more pertinent to our story here, like a good director who pulls back the curtain for the next scene when we thought the play was just about over.

A lot happens behind the scenes. The more I walk with God, the more I realize just how many acts He has written into my life's screenplay. Often when I think a scene is about over, God is setting the stage for an encore.

An encore is a repeated or an additional performance. I don't always think of repetition as exciting. But I do believe that it's in the mundane day-to-day living that we are being developed and God's purposes are played out. We have to be diligent about being alert and awake to what God has planned and what He wants of us, or our days can woo us into a sleep even though our eyes appear to be open.

By now, Esther was queen and living her daily life alongside her husband, King Ahasuerus. Her guardian, Mordecai, was keeping his eye on her by hanging out at the city gate. Meanwhile, a snake named Haman slithered next to Esther's hubby and got appointed to be his right-hand man. He was even given the emperor's ring to wear as a sign of his power.

Notice the backstage script. If we are not careful, we can think that what we have or where we are positioned in life is solely for our own purposes. Esther went from an orphan to adoption to being planted as a queen in a prominent kingdom to throw confetti for a specific purpose.

No one had ever asked Esther her ethnic background. When it turned out Haman hated Jews, Esther was set up to be an answer to a huge problem.

Everyone had to bow down to Haman. When Mordecai refused, Haman became livid. When he discovered Mordecai was Jewish, he went ballistic.

> When Haman saw [this], he was filled with rage. And when he learned of Mordecai's ethnic identity it seemed repugnant for Haman to do away with Mordecai alone. He planned to destroy all of Mordecai's people, the Jews, throughout Ahasuerus's kingdom. (Esther 3:5-6 CSB)

Haman convinced King Ahasuerus to decree the ethnic cleansing of all the Jews throughout his empire. Mordecai heard the awful announcement and asked Esther to intervene with her husband, sending her these beautiful words:

> Who knows, perhaps you have come to your royal position for such a time as this. (Esther 4:14 CSB)

Mordecai was as responsible for saving his people as Esther was. Both were set up by God to accomplish His purposes. Sometimes it will be our job to speak and champion people, and sometimes it will be our job to inspire another person to speak and take a stand.

RULING & WAITING

Esther understood the importance of timing. She knew she needed to address the king and use words that would persuade him.
She was in a 9-1-1 situation.

Haman was building an awful machine for ethnic cleansing.
Some translations say a pole for impaling; some say a gallows for
hanging. But at seventy-five feet high (see Esther 5:14), it's clear
Haman's rage against the Jews was in full fury.

Yet Esther waited three whole days so that her people could fast
and pray on her behalf. When it becomes obvious that there is
something we need to say or do, let's learn from the queen. Let's
take the time to ask God for His wisdom and make room for Him
to work. That way when we have to take our place and say the
thing, He has already prepared the way for us.

Meanwhile, the king happened to be restless back at the palace.
In the middle of the night, the king was up reading reports of
the day's activities because, funny enough, he wasn't able to
sleep. That is where he read about Esther's guardian, Mordecai,
and how he had done the king a great favor by telling him of an
assassination plot.

A lot happens between chapters 4 and 10 in the book of Esther.
Esther was granted permission to come and be with the king.
She asked for his help to intervene. Then step by step Haman's
schemes against her people unfolded. I have to say it is brilliant.

Haman ended up being hung on the gallows he had built for the Jews, and Mordecai was promoted in the palace and his fame spread throughout the kingdom. Sometimes what we want for our enemies can end up on our own heads.

Esther's favor got her all the way to the king's palace, but not so that she could relax and sip margaritas. God strategically positioned her to save her people. She was a chosen voice of *hooray* to help a people doomed to misfortune unless God stepped in and did something.

I'm sensing that the stage has been set in America to deal with ethnic/racial injustices similar to those of Esther's time. God is in the business of placing each of us in just the right position "for such a time as this." We need to use our voices and privileges and positions to help those in our communities who are being squelched.

God's solution is us. He uses our lives as vehicles to transport change. When we partner with God to be *hooray* for others, the plans of the enemy can be stopped and people can be helped.

Not every setup is for a watching world, of course. Sometimes the sweetest setups are shared privately between you and God or you and others. There is not a situation that God hasn't written a new scene for, and like with Esther, He will use the stages we stand on and the places He puts us for a grander purpose—to be a hope and a help.

GETTING WHAT WE DIDN'T ASK FOR

It is an incredible thing when we go to the king (a real ruler, a metaphorical one, or the King of Kings Himself) and, like Esther, we get what we ask for. It's another kind of incredible when we don't go to our King to ask for anything, yet God sees fit to be generous with us.

In 2 Kings 4 there is a story of "a prominent woman" (csb) who wasn't asking for anything but, like Esther, found herself in the middle of a setup. Sometimes our setups are about saving others, and sometimes they are about saving us.

We are never told this woman's name; she's only referred to as the Shunammite woman. But her story is still being told today because her choice to serve created a legacy worth retelling.

The Shunammite woman showed incredible generosity toward a prophet named Elisha. She had an eye for what he was doing and watched him traveling back and forth. She spotted some needs and came up with a way to meet those needs and serve the man of God.

> She said to her husband, "I know that the one who often passes by here is a holy man of God, so let's make a small, walled-in upper room and put a bed, a table, a chair, and a lamp there for him." (2 Kings 4:9-10 csb)

Her kind hospitality motivated Elisha to offer her something in return. He suggested that he speak to the king on her behalf. However, the woman basically said she was already content and didn't need anything from him. Wow, that's confetti, friends. When we serve and give without wanting anything in return, confetti is being thrown in its purest form.

Thankfully, Elisha didn't leave it at that. He listened to God, and his servant Gehazi. In fact, Elisha requested advice from Gehazi, who was sensitive enough to recognize the Shunammite woman's deepest need.

> Elisha asked Gehazi, "What can we do for her?"
> Gehazi replied, "She doesn't have a son, and her husband is an old man." (2 Kings 4:14 NLT)

Then Elisha extended to the woman a big statement of *hooray*, a promised word from the Lord: "At this time next year you will have a son in your arms" (2 Kings 4:16 CSB).

I love Elisha's boldness and courage to prophesy about a baby and then state a timeline to a woman he barely knew. I also love his willingness to be the mouthpiece for God. We want to get around people who have credibility when it comes to accurate prophetic words and powerful miracles.

We have the opportunity to become those same kinds of people. God doesn't choose favorites. We can all have as much of Him or as little as we want. "For God gives the Spirit without limit" (John 3:34). Our intentionality with Scripture, the Holy Spirit, worship, and prayer is wide open for our own history making and confetti throwing.

MAKE THE FIRST MOVE

I want to point out that the Shunammite woman made the first move to bless. She put herself in front of Elisha and took action to serve, cook, buy, and build for him. She saw a need, served the need, and later reaped a harvest because of it. She multiplied what she had, not only for Elisha but also unknowingly for herself.

We can throw confetti from a distance, but it tends to land better when we are close. I wonder how many of us are looking for people to serve. Are we strategically going out of our way to support their cause? What if we went looking to bless and support others before they even asked for it? It's hard for people to ask for help. I rarely hear the ones in need saying, "Hey, how about you throw something my way for a while?"

What a thing to be able to have an eye for another while you are busy trying to help others. Everyone needs an advocate. God placed Elisha on a path that would walk him in front of this woman's house time and time again. Who is on your path?

Selfish ambition aside, it seems that the way to get what we want is to give to others what they need. When we take care of others, God takes care of us. If someone keeps showing up or walking by, ask yourself today, or rather ask God today, how you can bless them.

HOW MUCH DOES IT COST?

I find it interesting that the Bible story leaves out the price the Shunammite woman had to pay to feed and shelter Elisha. Maybe the general message is that it will cost us to see and serve. Jesus doesn't hold back when He tells us that we must count the cost before we become His disciples (see Luke 14:25-33). What a thing to ponder: a lot is required.

Generosity and hospitality do cost. They take our time, usually our finances, sometimes physical or emotional efforts.

Costly giving mustn't stop us from selfless serving. When we walk with God, we forfeit the option to hold back and hold on to what we perceive as "ours." The Apostle Paul says that we are to "share with the Lord's people who are in need. Practice hospitality" (Romans 12:13).

We get good at what we practice, for better or for worse. What we rehearse will become our patterns, and those patterns become habits in our lives. It would be helpful to stop and ask ourselves at different times if we like the patterns we're setting with our lives. Let's be the kind of people who practice creativity with our resources when it comes to our care, our share, and our cheer.

IT'S NOT A SETBACK, IT'S A SETUP

I've been in conversations with the Lord over things I didn't ask for, yet He gave—and then took away. Have you? It's hard to birth something you've asked for; it's just as hard to birth what you didn't ask for, because once it's in your "womb," the promised thing becomes a part of you. Whether or not we know the reasons for the ending doesn't take away the grief.

At the same time, losing something precious almost always opens up a way for new growth. What does the story of the Shunammite woman and her son tell us about new beginnings and the miraculous?

Remember that when Elisha prophesied that the woman would bear a child, she basically told him not to mess with her. She didn't have the capacity to get her hopes up and then be let down.

> "No, my lord!" she cried. "O man of God, don't deceive me and get my hopes up like that." (2 Kings 4:16 NLT)

But Elisha's word proved true, and the baby grew into a boy. One day, working in the field with his father, he seemed to have an awful headache. His dad sent him home to his mom. The boy climbed into her lap and died.

Gulp, here's where we hold our breath. The woman had made it clear to the man of God that the seed of hope he was planting was serious business, and he had better be careful because her heart could not bear to move from content to hopeful. Now that seed was lying motionless, lying in her lap.

What did the devastated mother do next? She carried the boy upstairs and laid him on Elisha's bed. (Such a touching detail!) Then she kicked her holy boldness into full throttle, raced to the man of God, and demanded a miracle.

> "Did I ask you for a son, my lord? And didn't I say, 'Don't deceive me and get my hopes up'?" (2 Kings 4:28 NLT)

I love that this woman knew that a person of God should be able to help her. My theological tradition teaches that modern-day believers should be able to make the same requests and see the answers. The book of Acts doesn't have an ending in the Bible, and when napkins, aprons, and shadows are healing people because the Holy Spirit is doing something, we can get our hopes up because He is the same one who works with us today.

Of course, not all things that die in our lives get to be resurrected, but they certainly have no chance if we aren't persistent in our pursuit about something that needs to be done.

Elisha went to the boy and worked and worked until a miracle happened. The boy was revived, and God was glorified. The mother, overwhelmed with gratitude, fell at his feet and bowed before him. Then she took her son in her arms and carried him downstairs (see 2 Kings 4:36-37).

It was just another day for Elisha. The supernatural was just natural living to him. I love being around people like that.

I can only imagine what the woman was thinking and what kind of prayers she was praying as she made her way toward the man of God for help. We don't always know when and how God is setting the stage for a miracle to take place. I propose that it was God Who caused her eye to notice the man on her path to begin with, and when she chose to serve Elisha's needs, that was the beginning of her setup. Her opportunity didn't look like much, just a simple gesture to provide a man of God with comfort while he worked. She was looking to help the man of God, and all the while God was looking to help her.

The resurrection of her son was at least her third miracle. I doubt it would be her last. If God has done something for you, He can do it again. He builds trust and history with us by being consistent in our lives. He is good and faithful, and He won't have any problem if you ask Him to prove it to you.

Confetti fell that day. I imagine it left a trail all the way back home as she rode her donkey and held her boy. Let's keep our promises close in this season and not settle for less than God wants to give us.

Meditation

I wonder how many of us have been disappointed by promises that have fallen to the ground, or have been disappointed with God because something didn't turn out the way we expected.

God often has unique, sometimes strange (to us) ways of showing up. But He does show up. Confetti comes for us, and *hooray* helps us get back up on our feet.

So with that in mind, let's ponder some thoughts:
- In the meantime, who might He be putting in your path to notice, to help, or to serve?
- Are there any promises in your life that need to be resurrected?

REFLECTION

When the LORD restored the fortunes of Zion, we were like those who dream. Our mouths were filled with laughter then, and our tongues with shouts of joy. Then they said among the nations, "The LORD has done great things for them." The LORD has done great things for us; we were joyful. Restore our fortunes, LORD, like watercourses in the Negev. Those who sew in tears will reap with shouts of joy. (Psalm 126:1-5 CSB)

EPILOGUE

Dear reader, you have now seen all the different ways confetti can be thrown. It's my hope that after reading this, you will adapt or invent your own way to *become a voice of hooray in a hurting world.*

You won't know what good it can do until you offer it. God has put something inside each of us that is to be shared with the world. It's something that can only be offered by you. It's not less than what others have, and it's not better than what they carry. It's just uniquely yours, and it's needed for right now.

In the Apostle Paul's words,

> Love one another deeply as brothers and sisters. Take the lead in honoring one another. Do not lack diligence in zeal; be fervent in the Spirit; serve the Lord. . . . Share with the saints in their needs; pursue hospitality. Bless those who persecute you; bless and do not curse. Rejoice with those who rejoice; weep with those who weep. Live in harmony with one another. (Romans 12:10-11, 13-16 CSB)

May *hooray* be on your lips and confetti in your heart.

—*DeAnn Carpenter*

ENDNOTES

[1] This quote is often erroneously attributed to Maya Angelou. https://quoteinvestigator.com/2014/04/06/they-feel/.

[2] Marianne Williamson, *A Return to Love: Reflections on the Principles of 'A Course in Miracles'* (New York: HarperCollins, 1996), 165.

[3] Attributed without support. No one knows who first said it. Cf., https://essentialcslewis.com/2017/11/11/ccslq-41-go-back-and-change/; https://quoteinvestigator.com/2015/11/05/new-ending/; https://www.cslewis.com/surprised-by-misquotes/.

[4] J. R. R. Tolkien, *The Two Towers: Being the Second Part of The Lord of the Rings* (New York: Ballantine Books, 1965), 152.

THANK YOU

Brian: My favorite husband, I wouldn't even understand *hooray* if you didn't model it for me every single day. You are the very best person I know. I love you dearly.

Asher and Ruby: You are my favorite people to cheer for . . . you always will be. My pom-poms will always be ready. I love and adore you SO GOSH DARN MUCH it hurts sometimes. Always keep confetti with you. I know it won't be hard for you.

Ginger Simmons: I am forever indebted to and marked by your wisdom, rebuke, encouragement, and love. Thanks for being such a great teacher, friend, and fan. Thank you also for trusting both my heart and my voice enough to give it a platform so I could share the things of God. I love you.

My cheering section: Jess, Brooke, Dawn, Sarah, Brandi, Jenna, Maggie, Brittany, my Refuge team. Thank you. I live not only by His Word, but by the words we share as He reveals them to us. It takes strength to hold each other's arms high, and I am always so happy to help hold yours. We are a lucky bunch.

P.S. Dawn: Your embodiment of *hooray* has been a constant example to me from the day I met you. Your cheer is both rare and wonderful; thank you for holding up your megaphone.

My sisters: People really can change! Thanks for sticking by me and not letting our past dictate our future. Kendra, I might not be writing if you weren't so persistent; no older sister is as lucky. Alyssa, your megaphone is your servanthood, and it's as loud as ever. I love you both dearly.

Mom and Dad: Who'd have thought God would use this quick tongue and charming personality? HA! I don't tell you enough what great parents you are! Thanks for your constant love and support . . . and for not squelching all that God has wanted from us. I'm sure it's been like watching a roller-coaster ride. Your neck probably hurts, but you've been great fans.

Lastly, to Tom, Ann, and Tim: Thank you for taking God's assignments seriously. Young Life has marked my life. I am (along with so many others) forever indebted to your obedience and sacrifice to serve the mission for which Christ came. Your love and extension of the Good News changed me. I am eternally grateful.

ABOUT THE AUTHOR

DeAnn Carpenter writes, teaches, and serves because she's passionate about supporting and celebrating others. Together she and her husband, Brian Carpenter, founded and direct the nonprofit, Refuge Foundation. (See https://Refuge.Rest.) They reside in Montana with their two kids, Asher and Ruby. There they train and develop staff to care for, serve, and support leaders.

Refuge is currently in multiple locations in the American West, bringing reprieve and rest to leaders from all over the world. DeAnn helps with staff development and directs the Refuge W.I.L.D. experience (see http://RefugeWild.org), which guides women toward deeper living with God and with one another.

DeAnn grew up in the Great Plains of North Dakota before moving to Montana. In Montana she attended the Yellowstone Valley Bible Institute, where she worked on staff serving youth, young adults, and women's ministries. She has flipped many houses, worked in the salon industry, taught at women's conferences, and will always be "in the business of transformation."

She spends her free time running around with her kids, sipping coffee, reading books, hanging with her girlfriends, and eating Thai food with her family.

Reach out to DeAnn on her website: www.DeAnnCarpenter.com.